Grafton Regis

Grafton Regis

The History of a Northamptonshire Village

Edited by
Charles FitzRoy
and Keith Harry

MERTON PRIORY PRESS

First published 2000

Published by Merton Priory Press Ltd
67 Merthyr Road, Whitchurch
Cardiff CF14 1DD

ISBN 1 898937 41 9

*Dedicated to the Memory of
Ken Plummer (1935–1998)
whose love and enthusiasm
for the history of Grafton Regis
was the inspiration for this book*

Printed by Hillman Printers (Frome) Ltd
Handlemaker Road, Marston Trading Estate
Frome, Somerset, BA11 4RW

CONTENTS

LIST OF ILLUSTRATIONS

Black and White

Colour Plates

Between pages 106 and 107

ILLUSTRATION ACKNOWLEDGEMENTS

Don Allen: 39, 48
Ena Atkins: 44
Peter Blake: 37
A.E. Brown: 3–10
Doreen Cann: 40
Chronicle & Echo, Northampton: 49
Mrs Margaret Colgrove: Colour Plate 11
Charles FitzRoy: 50
Barry Glanville: 31, 45, Colour Plate 10
The Duke of Grafton KG. Courtesy of the Photographic Survey, Courtauld Institute of Art: 18, 22–26, 28, 29, 31
Mary Grout: 2, 32, 34, 38, 46
David Hall: 13, 27
Mike John: 33, 36
John Rylands University of Manchester Library: 35
Ministry of Defence. Crown Copyright: Colour Plate 12
National Monuments Record. Crown Copyright: 12
National Portrait Gallery, London: 15, 17, Colour Plate 1
Northamptonshire Record Office: Colour Plates 6–9
Northamptonshire County Library: 1
Northamptonshire Heritage: 21
Queens' College, Cambridge. Reproduced by permission of the President and Fellows of the College: Colour Plate 2.
Siege Group: 19, 20
Thyssen-Bornemisza Museum, Madrid: Colour Plate 3
Joan Ward: 42, 43, 51, 52
Joy Wilson: 41, 47

SUBSCRIBERS

Leonard Abrey, Northwood (Middle-sex)
Peter and Christine Adams, Hartwell
Rupert and Mark Adams, Cosgrove
Dr John Adamson, Cambridge
Mr C.J. and Mrs M.M. Addington, Pinner (Middlesex)
P. and P.D. Addington, Brixworth
John V. Addis-Smith, Thurleigh (Beds.)
James and Celestria Alexander-Sinclair, Towcester
Carol Allen, Willesborough Lees (Kent)
Don Allen, Alderton
Mrs Joyce Allen, Grafton Regis
Linda J. Allen, Northampton
Ron Allen, New Duston
Mrs Florence Allen, St Austell (Cornwall)
Maurice Allen, Ross-on-Wye (Herefs.)
Paul Allen, Shutlanger
Ruth Amedelle JP, Northolt (Middlesex)
P.J. Andrews, Nether Heyford
Alec Annand, Midhurst (Sussex)
Mr and Mrs David Apperly, Wicken
Derek and Iris Appleby, Roade
Mr S.R. Appleby and Mrs L.J.M. Collier, Yardley Gobion
Mr and Mrs Craig Ardrey, Bicester (Oxon.)
W.P. Asbrey, Kettering
Douglas Ashby, Burton Latimer
Ian Askew, Wellingham (Sussex)
Robert Ayers, Northampton

Peter Baines, Buckingham
Sonia Baker, Grafton Regis
Mrs Vivienne Baker, Towcester

Julie Barrie and David Hartley, Cald-ecote
J. Bazeley, Euxton (Lancs.)
Judith Beattie, West Melton, Victoria (Australia)
Nicholas and Laura Beatty, Chicheley (Bucks.) *(2 copies)*
Chloë and Luke Beauchamp, Yardley Gobion
Darrell Peter Benge, Yardley Gobion
Tracy Leigh Benge, Yardley Gobion
Betty Kathleen Bennie, Roade
Simon and Marianne Bicket, Blis-worth
Bidwells Property Consultants, North-ampton
Vivien Billington, Bath
Mrs Gary Black, Shefford Woodlands (Berks.)
Margaret V. and Adam J.I. Blacklay, Milton Keynes (Bucks.)
Giles and Marcus Blake, Grafton Regis
Peter and Sue Blake, Grafton Regis *(2 copies)*
Mrs M.N. Blincow, Roade
Benjamin and Marcia Blunt, Whit-field, Queensland (Australia)
Daniel Blunt and Wendy Brown, Whitfield, Queensland (Australia)
Teresa Blunt, Whitfield, Queensland (Australia)
Andrew Bonar, Grafton Regis
Hilary and Peter Bonar, Grafton Regis
Arnold G.W. Boon, Gretton
Michael Boon, Grafton Regis
Samantha Boon, Great Linford (Bucks.)
Tim Boswell MP, Aynho

Ruth and Ernie Bowden, Stony
  Stratford (Bucks.)
Mrs Yvonne Brain, Corby
Peter F. Brazell, Stony Stratford
  (Bucks.)
Tony, Maureen and Nozomi Briggs,
  Stanbridge (Beds.)
Barbara and David Brogden, Milton
  Malsor
Andrée M. Brown, Ashton
Mr Ian and Mrs Jo Brown, Towcester
Ernie Bryant, Wollaston
Peter and Norma Bull, Blisworth
Eric and Brenda Burgess, Wolverton
Amanda and David Burton, North-
  ampton
Michael and Lorraine Bywater,
  Potterspury

Jeremy Calderwood, Harpole
Mrs Doreen Mary Cann (née
  Morton), Towcester
Brian John Carter, Milton Malsor
Mr R.J. Carter, Monks Risborough
  (Bucks.) *(2 copies)*
Sarah Castle and Becky Castle, Graf-
  ton Regis *(2 copies)*
Edmund D.P. and Gloria T. Caws,
  Hartwell
R.D. Chancellor, Stoke Bruerne
Ray Chaplin, Towcester
Mrs Edna Chapman, Northampton
The Ven. Michael Chapman, Arch-
  deacon of Northampton, North-
  ampton
Dave and Mary Chappell, Rushden
Dr M.J. Chappell, Coventry *(2
  copies)*
Roger and Sheila Charlton, Milton
  Malsor
Mr Edwin L. Cherry, Cheriton
  (Hants.)
Linda and Mike Chew, Weston Favell
Dorothy and Denis Chipperfield,
  Stony Stratford (Bucks.)
Ken and Helen Chitty, Grafton Regis
Jack D. and Doris R. Clamp, Greens
  Norton

Daphne M. Clark, Melksham (Wilts.)

Paul and Jackie Clayton, Alderton
Reginald and Doris Clifford,
  Northampton
Noreen Clydesdale, Northampton
John Coales, Somerton (Somerset)
John and Margaret Colgrove, Grafton
  Regis
Tony and Kathy Colgrove, Grafton
  Regis
Brian and Janet Collings, Stoke
  Bruerne
Barry and Nicola (née Rogers)
  Collins, Stamford (Lincs.)
Rachael Collins, Grafton Regis
Deborah and Andrew Colvill, Great
  Linford (Bucks.)
Dr R.F.B. Conlon, Stoke Bruerne
Pat and Mercia Cooper, Stoke
  Bruerne
David and Sheila Coote, Alderton
Jane Ann and Jennifer Clare Corrin,
  Yardley Gobion
Jill and Derek Cornwell, Stoke Bru-
  erne
Peter, Sally, Sarah and Michael Cos-
  ford, Collingtree
The Revd Dr J.M. Courtie, Blisworth
Alan Cowie, London
Elizabeth Cowie, Buckie (Banffs.)
Wendy Cox, Stoke Bruerne
Colin and Shirley Coxall, Chipstead
  (Surrey)
Edward Crawfurd, Paulerspury
Dennis James Cripps, Marsh Gibbon
  (Oxon.)
Mrs Betty U. Crisp (née Dewick),
  Maidenhead (Berks.)
David and Linda Currie, Cullen
  (Banffs.)
Robert Curley, Yardley Gobion

Julia H. and Sidney William Dale
  Skinner, Yardley Gobion
Paul and Linda Dards, Alderton
Canon C.H. Davidson and the Revd
  R.P. Cave, Roade *(2 copies)*

The Davison Family, Potterspury
Edward T. Dawkins, Northampton
Bernard Day, Ashton
Clare and Stephen Dennis, Colling-
tree *(2 copies)*
Norman Denny and Emrys Brooks,
Stoke Bruerne *(2 copies)*
Graham and Yvonne Denny, Thetford
(Suffolk)
Mr and Mrs S.G. Dimmock, Grafton
Regis
Raymond Dines, Hartwell
Mrs J.M. Domhof, Scaldwell
Eric and Alison Douglas, Aberdeen
Michael Dowden, Roade
Cara Leigh and John Alan Drake,
Grafton Regis *(2 copies)*
Les Drake and Joan Drake, Grafton
Regis *(2 copies)*
B.J. and F.G. Draper, Middleton-on-
Sea (Sussex)
Bill and Dee Dredge, Roade
Mr D. and Mrs J. Drewett, Yardley
Gobion
Cathie Drewitt, Alderton
Paul Drewitt, Alderton *(10 copies)*
Mrs Kay Drewitt, Beverley (Yorks.)
Mr W.T. Duncan, Potterspury
Mr Alex Dunkley, Kingsthorpe
Derrick Durham, Hardingstone

Susan and Trevor Earl, Paulerspury
Mrs A.M. and Miss J.A. Eales, Old
Stratford
Michael and Betty East, Gayton
The Eckles Family, Bridlington
(Yorks.)
Barbara J. Edwards (née Addington)
and E.H.J. Edwards, London
Bill Edwards, Luton (Beds.)
David Victor Edwards, Hartwell
Mr B.S.H. Egan, Stony Stratford
(Bucks.)
Mrs Gwenyth Eggleton,
Irthlingborough
Lady Alethea Eliot, Leominster
(Herefs.)
K.R. Embleton, Syresham

The Earl and Countess of Euston,
Euston (Suffolk) *(6 copies)*
John J. Evans, Northampton
R. and J. Evans, Shutlanger

Peter and Eileen Fair, Flore
David and Delia Farrand, Ashton
Harry and Jean Farrow, Grafton
Regis
Jenifer Fell, Hellidon
A.B.X. Fenwick, Sholebroke
David and Margaret Fitzhugh, Stoke
Bruerne
Charles and Diana FitzRoy, Grafton
Regis
Nicholas and George FitzRoy,
Grafton Regis
Barbara and Ted Flack, Yardley
Gobion
Margaret Forrest, Upper Harlestone
Oliver George and Archie William
Forsyth, Pury End
Donna and Graham Fossey,
Thelnetham (Norfolk)
George and Miranda Fountaine,
Grafton Regis
Clive and Barbara Fox, Grafton Regis
(3 copies)
Dorothy and Ron Freeman, Milton
Keynes (Bucks.)
Len and Betty Freeman, Wicken
George Freeston, Blisworth
G. and S. Freestone, Cosgrove
Jane Froome (née Gower), Corby
Jayne and Peter Frost, Blisworth

Mrs Eileen Gabriel, Blisworth
Prince Yuri Galitzine, Stamford
(Lincs.)
John and Sheila Gallimore, Grafton
Regis
Neil Gallop, Darmstädt (Germany)
Mr and Mrs R. Gallop, Newport
Pagnell (Bucks.)
H.M. Gardner, Dunchurch
(Warwicks.)
Robert and Sue Gardner, Stoke
Bruerne

Ann Garfield, Alvaston (Derbys.)
Miss J.M. Garland, London
Alan and David Garman, Fakenham Magna (Suffolk)
Jane and Michael Garrod, Thelnetham (Norfolk)
Sheila Gee, Paulerspury
Lord and Lady Gibson, Tunbridge Wells (Kent)
Verena Gibson, Northampton
Brian Giggins, Towcester
Richard and Joyce Gilbert, Wicken
John Abbott Gilson, Roade
Barry and Jean Glanville, Grafton Regis *(4 copies)*
Val Glover, Towcester
Mr Edwin and Mrs Vera Glynn, Northampton
Jay and Guy Goble, Grafton Regis *(2 copies)*
Mr and Mrs S. Goble, Grafton Regis *(2 copies)*
Chris Godbold and Trevor Haynes, Corby
Barbara and Barry Goodman, Old Stratford *(2 copies)*
Mr and Mrs Campbell Gordon, London
Toni Gordon, Watford (Herts.)
Jack Gould, Harleston (Norfolk)
S.J. Goulding, Yardley Gobion
The Duke of Grafton KG, Euston (Suffolk) *(3 copies)*
The Duchess of Grafton GCVO, Euston (Suffolk) *(2 copies)*
Staff and Residents of Grafton Manor, Grafton Regis
Mrs Eva Green and Mrs Shirley Buckland (née Green), Roade
Mr R.J. Green, Christchurch (New Zealand)
Anthea Greenaway and Timothy J. Dumpleton, Blakeney (Gloucs.)
Mrs K. Greenhouse, San Miguel de Allende (Mexico)
Ray and Joyce Grimes, Northampton
Mrs Mary Grout (née Annand), Cambridge

David Grout, Worcester Park (Surrey)
Michael Grout, Queenscliffe, Victoria (Australia)
Timothy Grout, Cambridge

Elizabeth Hall, Stoke Bruerne
Robert and Daryl Halsey, Alderton
R.H. Hanson, Princes Risborough (Bucks.)
Ian and Loredana Harley, Milton Malsor *(2 copies)*
A. and Sue Harris, Old Stratford
David Harris and Lynn Harris, Wellingborough
Joan Harris, Harborne (Warwicks.)
John Harris, Hardingstone *(2 copies)*
Roger R. Harris, Roade
Miss Mona C. Harrison, Northampton
James William and Ashleigh Clare Harrod, Grafton Regis
Keith and Kathy Harry, Grafton Regis
May Harry, Dobwalls (Cornwall)
The Hart Family, Shenley Brook End (Bucks.)
Ellen Mary and William Douglas Hart, Yardley Gobion
Mrs Anne Hartley-Schilt, Enschede (Netherlands)
Peter J. Hawkins, Ringwood North, Victoria (Australia)
Pierston J. Hawkins, Ringwood North, Victoria (Australia)
Raglan J.F. Hawkins, Ringwood North, Victoria (Australia)
Tamor P. Hawkins, Ringwood North, Victoria (Australia)
Douglas Hawtin, Northampton
Malcolm Hay, Huntly (Aberdeenshire)
Julia Haynes, Yardley Gobion
Mr and Mrs K.S. Hayward, Yardley Gobion
Christian, Lady Hesketh, Easton Neston
George and Jean Hickford, Northampton
Canon Jack Higham, Peterborough

Virginia and Roger Hill, Brampford Speke (Devon)

Peter Hillson, King's Heath (Birmingham)

Mrs Rosemary Hinton, Lois Weedon

Mr and Mrs W.J.K. Hoare, North Garden, Virginia (USA)

David Hogan and Fanny Bradbury, Brighton (Sussex)

Robert Holden, Sibdon (Salop)

Mr G. Holding, Paulerspury

P.R. and S. Holloway, Grafton Regis *(3 copies)*

Dr Steven Hollowell, Cogenhoe

Reginald Hubert and Irene Margaret Holman, Grafton Regis

Mr and Mrs A.L. Holton, Yardley Gobion

Mrs Olive M. Holton, Helmdon

Barry and Gill Horn, Yardley Gobion

Teresa and Tony Horner, Kingsthorpe

David Hornsey, Kettering

Bridget Howard and Derek Batten, Paulerspury

Hazel and Bill Howell, Greens Norton

John and Beryl Howell, St Ives, New South Wales (Australia)

David and Frances Howell, Southam (Warwicks.)

John Edward Hudson, Paris (France)

Mrs Cicely E. Hughes, Weedon Bec

Hazel and Kevin Hughes, Towcester

Keira and Oliver Hughes, Towcester *(2 copies)*

William H. Hulme, Kettering

Mrs Dorothy Humphrey and Mrs Dorothy Hill, Quinton *(2 copies)*

John and Bertha Humphreys, Hartwell

Richard Paul Humphreys and Yvonne Hefford, Hartwell

Dennis Humphries and Dusty Roades, Towcester *(2 copies)*

Mrs M.D. Hunter, Ashton

Gillian Huntrods, Broughton Moor (Cumb.)

Tracey and Steve Illing, Great Linford (Bucks.)

Henry and Winifred Ivings, Euston (Suffolk) *(2 copies)*

Q. Jackson-Stops, Wood Burcote

T. Jackson-Stops, Wood Burcote

Christine James, Duston

Mrs Jean James, Stoke Bruerne

Enid Jarvis, Spratton

Donald and Katie Jaycock, Roade

Alanah and Tony Jeffries, Yardley Gobion

Colin and Sheila Jelley, Amersham (Bucks.) *(2 copies)*

Ronald J. Jelley, Amersham (Bucks.)

Alison and John Jenkins, Crowland (Lincs.)

Magnus and Martha John, Stony Stratford (Bucks.)

Marette I.B. John, Withington (Lancs.)

Nadia John, Wolverton (Bucks.)

Mrs Joan Johnson (née Allen), St Austell (Cornwall)

Mr and Mrs Bernard Jones, Stoke Bruerne

Don and Pam Jones, Deanshanger

Keith Judge, Long Lawford (Warwicks.)

Joy and Allan Kane, Barrie, Ontario (Canada)

Sherry Kane and Shaun Nicholls, Yardley Gobion

Jennifer Katzka, Washington DC (USA)

Mike Kelcey, Great Linford (Bucks.)

Margaret Kentigern-Fox, Raunds

Colin Kightley, Cosgrove

Donald Kightley and Beryl Kightley (née Tew), Church Brampton

Chris and Barbara King, Yardley Gobion

Patrick I. King, Boncath (Pembs.)

Suzanne King, Yardley Gobion

Matthew and Sybella Kirkbride, Bishopstone (Herefs.)

John S. Kliene, Alderton
Mrs K.M. Knight, Rushden
John and Doris Knights, Alderton
Mr K.J. and Mrs P. Knowles, Grafton
    Regis

Ann Lamb, Ashton
Audrey and Jim Lambert, Stony
    Stratford (Bucks.)
Maurice R. Lambert, Potterspury
Jim and Eilean Lavelle, Grafton
    Regis *(2 copies)*
Fiona and Anna Lavelle, Grafton
    Regis
Joan Leach, Llanyre (Rads.)
Robin Leleux, Wellingborough
Jean and David Lewis, Bridport
    (Dorset)
J.R. Lewis, Great Houghton
R.F. Lewis, Great Houghton
T.F. Lewis, Great Houghton
Anthony Neville and Valerie K.
    Linnell, Blisworth
Mrs S.M. Linnell, Hardingstone
Mr John and the Revd Susan Litch-
    field, Pury End
Alec and David Lovell, Olney
    (Bucks.) *(2 copies)*
Mary and Anetta Long, Blisworth
E.Y. Lynham and L. Freeland,
    Yardley Gobion
Rob and Linda Lyon, Milton Malsor

James and Linda McCormack,
    Grafton Regis
Patrick McCormack, Grafton Regis
Andy and Beryl McGookin, Milton
    Keynes (Bucks.)
Andrew, Monique and Edward
McGrath, Grafton Regis
Andy and Claire McGrath, Grafton
    Regis
Stuart and Betty McGrath, Kansas
    City, Kansas (USA)
Mrs Martin McLaren, Inkpen (Berks.)

Mr and Mrs R.G. Mackley,
    Northampton

Kathleen and David Maddock,
    Irthlingborough
Sheila and Tom Maddox, Yardley
    Gobion
Doug and Penny Madelin-Benger,
    Fornham All Saints (Suffolk)
Mrs A. Malin, Hartwell
Mrs Frances Betty Malton,
    Peterborough
John Marchant, Old Stratford
Brian W. and Samuel D. Martin,
    Grafton Regis *(2 copies)*
Judith A. Martin, Grafton Regis *(2
    copies)*
Robert and Kathryn Martin, Milden-
    hall (Suffolk)
Slim and Janet Mathews, Kettering
Dr Stephen Mattingly, Little Brington
The Revd David Maudlin, Radwinter
    (Essex)
Val and Tony Maycock, Blisworth
Alan George and Denise Anne
    Meakins, Potterspury
Nancy and Raymond William
    Meakins, Luton (Beds.)
Charlotte Metcalf, London
John and Daphne Metcalfe,
    Northampton
Mrs J. Miller-Stirling, Kenilworth,
    Cape Town (South Africa)
Shelley Mills, Bracknell (Berks.)
Gay and Cyril Millward, Stony
    Stratford
Milo Molloy and Denise Sparrow,
    Castlethorpe (Bucks.)
Jill and Jack Moore, Haywards Heath
    (Sussex)
Guy and Rose Monson, London *(3
    copies)*
Olivia and Leonora Monson, London
    (2 copies)
John V. Morison, Hallaton (Leics.)
Trevor Morley, Stoke Bruerne *(2
    copies)*
Shirley Morris, Roade
Mr Leslie Morton, South Harrow
    (Middlesex)
Joanna Moxham, Spratton

Trevor and Audrey Mynard, Wellingborough

Robert and Janet Newman, Cottingham
Kevin and Sue Nichols, Everdon
S.W. Nichols, Northampton
Julia Noikovitch, Leighton Buzzard (Beds.)
Chris and Joan Norman, Olney (Bucks.)
Northamptonshire Family History Society
Northamptonshire Heritage, Northampton
Lady Nutting, Chicheley (Bucks.)

Old Stratford County Primary School
Ian and Carole O'Neill, Edlesborough (Beds.)
Eva Onley (née Moreton), Wellingborough
Mr Brian (Ozzy) and Mrs Doreen Osborne, Hartwell
Jim and Pam Osborne, Higham Ferrers

Judy Padgett, Grafton Regis
Mr E. and Mrs K.M. Page, Burton-on-the-Wolds (Leics.)
Mark Page, Birmingham
Joan and Mike Paris, Castlethorpe (Bucks.)
Nikki Patterson, Grafton Regis
John and Mary Payne, Weston Favell
Jonathan Pearson, Castle Ashby
David Pease, Sherington (Bucks.)
Kathleen Peck, Helensburgh (Dunbartonshire)
A.E. Perkins, Northampton
Colin James Perridge, Ashley
David Pickering, Grafton Regis
Maureen Pitt, Dobwalls (Cornwall)
Les and Brenda Pittam, Yardley Gobion
Angela Plummer, Blisworth
Ron and Barbara Plummer, Northampton *(2 copies)*

Mark and Eirwen Pople, Towcester
Potterspury Lodge School, Potterspury
Stan Power, Liverpool (Lancs.)
Rita and Rod Poxon, Gayton
Lord Michael Pratt, London
The Baron of Prestoungrange and Lady Avril Wills, Milton Malsor
David and Pauline Probert, Alderton
Roger and Pat Pye, Potterspury

Rory Rae, London
Paul and Scott Rayson, Stoke Bruerne *(2 copies)*
Charles and Julie Reece, Grafton Regis
Mrs Hylda J. and Mr Clive Edward Reece, Grafton Regis *(2 copies)*
Helena Kate Reece, Grafton Regis
Jennifer Anne Reece and Oliver James Solan, Earls Barton
Louisa Jane Reece, Grafton Regis
Frederick George Rich and Dorothy Muriel Rich (née Addington), Chalfont St Peter (Bucks.)
Pat and Terry Richardson, Potterspury
C.W. Richmond-Watson, Paulerspury
Mr and Mrs R.N. Richmond-Watson, Potterspury
Sarah and Julian Richmond-Watson, Potterspury
Stuart Richmond-Watson, Potterspury *(2 copies)*
Marcelle Ridout, Peppard Common (Oxon.)
Victoria and Danielle Riley, Willoughby (Warwicks.)
Ian and Heather Ritchie, Hanslope (Bucks.)
Michael Robbins, Teddington (Mddx)
Norman Robinson, Woodstock (Oxon.)
Phyllis Robinson, Earls Barton
Jeremiah Rogers, Grafton Regis
Robin and Judith Rogers, Stamford (Lincs.)
Phil Roper and Rachel Smith, Grafton Regis *(8 copies)*

Charles and Susan Rose, Badby
Mrs Eileen and Mr Robert Rose, New
 Duston
Mrs M.M. Rowden, Boughton
P.E.J. Rowden, Eastcote
Phyllis Russell, Potterspury

Edward and Henrietta St George,
 London *(5 copies)*
David Saint and Dennis Wiles
 Cloves, Wellingborough
Mr and Mrs Michael Sakkalli,
 Plumpton
Mr Joseph and Mrs Mary Sargeant,
 Grafton Regis
Mr Jeffrey Sargeant, Grafton Regis
Frank Saunders, Cosgrove
Philip and Diane Saunderson, Weston
 Favell
Gordon J. and Angela B. Semple,
 Lutterworth (Leics.)
Major Bruce Shand, Stourpaine
 (Dorset)
William Shearer, Church Brampton
Mr W.G.N. and Mrs M.I. Shears,
 Roade
Mr and Mrs G.P. Shelmardine,
 Yardley Gobion
Geoffrey W. and Muriel M Shepherd.
 Whittlebury
Jeanette Shore, Binfield (Berks.)
David M.V. and Juliet M. Short,
 Newton (Cambs.) *(2 copies)*
Brian and Joyce Shrigley, Wollaston
Judy, Martin, Benjamin and Adam
 Simons, Hanslope and Yardley
 Gobion *(2 copies)*
Mrs Jane Skinner (née Sargeant),
 Grafton Regis
Brenda R. Slack, Pury End
Derek Smeathers, Great Billing
Andrew and Joane Smith, Ashton
Barty Smith, White Waltham (Berks.)
David and Denise Smith, Buck-
 ingham
Grahame and Josie Smith, Ashton *(2
 copies)*

Hugo and Sophie Smith, Little Sax-
 ham (Suffolk)
J.F.E. Smith, Slaugham (Sussex) *(3
 copies)*
J.R.E. Smith, Balcombe (Sussex)
Jean Smith, Stony Stratford (Bucks.)
Julian Smith, Slaugham (Sussex)
Sir John Smith CH CBE, Maidenhead
 (Berks.)
Dr Peter J. and Mrs Aida S. Smith,
 Hanslope (Bucks.)
Capt. W.G. Smith VRD RNR (Ret'd)
 and Mrs Edith Doreen Smith,
 Willington (Beds.)
Wendy Smith, Grafton Regis
Bob and Ruth Snedker, Pury End
South Northamptonshire Council,
 Towcester
David and Yunita Speller, Bath
Christopher Spicer, Euston (Suffolk)
Sir James and Lady Spooner,
 Pytchley
Dr and Mrs J. Spurrier, Blisworth
Mr and Mrs Walter Stageman,
 Greatworth
Mr and Mrs W. Stenton, Yardley
 Gobion
Miss M.R. Stevens, Market
 Harborough (Leics.)
Wendy and Martin Storey, Shutlanger
Doris and Don Street, Albrighton
 (Salop)
Mr Michael J. and Mrs Josephine V.
 Streeton, Earls Barton
Josephine M. and Peter F.J. Strong,
 Bracknell (Berks.)
Dr John R. Sunderland, Towcester
David and Anne Sutcliffe, Camberley
 (Surrey)
Martin and Rosemary Swain,
 Towcester
Sue and André Szczepanek, Hartwell

J. Peter Tanswell, Blakesley
Mr K.R. Tattersall, Sulgrave
Alan M. Taylor and Carol A. Smith,
 Yardley Gobion *(2 copies)*
Barry and Elizabeth Taylor, Stanwick

Mrs E.K. (Jean) Taylor and Mrs Judy Cave, Stoke Bruerne *(2 copies)*

Felicity Taylor (née Annand) and Simon Annand, Reading (Berks.)

Melinda and Nicholas Taylor, Lillingstone Lovell (Bucks.)

Ioan and Alice Thomas, Oundle

Mr and Mrs Alan Thompson, Pulloxhill (Beds.)

Janette and David Leonard Thornton, Wormleighton (Warwicks.)

Brian M. Tipping, Tamworth (Staffs.)

Brian Tite, Grafton Regis

John T. and Pamela B. Todd, Long Buckby

Towcester and District Local History Society

Clare and Andrew Towers, Stoke Bruerne

The Rt. Hon. The Baroness Trumpington, London

Mr Peter and Mrs Brenda Trunk, Towcester

Chris and Patsy Turl, Yardley Gobion

Mr S.R. Turner, Stevenage (Herts.)

John and Jennifer Tustian, Silverstone

Mrs G.N. Underwood, Pitsford

R.P. and S. Underwood, Stoke Bruerne *(2 copies)*

Lois Vesty and Richard Hughes, Potterspury

E. Ruth Wagstaff, Chapel Brampton

Christine and Gerry Wainwright, Stoke Bruerne

Sir Hereward Wake Bt, Courteenhall

Mrs D.M. Walker and Mrs H. Tyrrell, Yardley Gobion

Rosemary Walker, Launton (Oxon.)

Joan Ward (née Elliott), Piddington

Vera Eileen Warner, Yardley Gobion

Jane S. and Terry Waterfield, Norton

David Watkin, Cambridge

Mr and Mrs E.G. Watson, Paulerspury *(2 copies)*

Mr and Mrs T.P. Watson, Ashton

Daphne and Jack Webb, Roade

Peter and Gill Webb, Potterspury

Raymond Webb and Mac Sharman, Old Stratford *(2 copies)*

Mr and Mrs N. Weeks, Yardley Gobion

Evelyn Weissenbach, Potterspury

Roy and Marion Welbourn, Longstanton (Cambs.)

Barbara A. West, Sheffield (Yorks.)

Raymond John and Janet Mary West, Towcester

Mr and Mrs R.W. Weston, Yardley Gobion

Richard and Carol Weston, Alderton *(2 copies)*

Paul Wheatcroft, Whitley (Lancs.)

Mark and Louise (née Rogers) Wheen, Stamford (Lincs.)

Mrs S. and Mr J. Whiley, Yardley Gobion

Jo White, Grafton Regis

Maureen White, Grafton Regis

Mrs Marie White, Clanfield (Hants.)

The Whiting Family, Milton Keynes (Bucks.)

Miss Myra Williams, Cambridge

Thomas Alan Williams and May Thorn, Old Haversham (Bucks.) *(2 copies)*

Fred and Barbara Willmer, Stony Stratford (Bucks.)

Andrea Wilson, Horsham (Sussex)

Dr Brian and Mrs Betty Wilson, Emberton (Bucks.)

Gilbert and Joy Wilson, Grafton Regis

Martin and Marion Wilson, Ashton

Robert and Janet Wilson, Hartwell

Nikki Woodward, Sandhurst (Berks.)

Wolverton and District Archaeological Society

Lyn and Trevor Woodger, Alderton

John and Vera Worledge, Northampton

Mr Maurice and Mrs Connie Wright, Roade

Frances Luczyc Wyhowska, London

CONTRIBUTORS TO
'GRAFTON REGIS SINCE 1900'

Don Allen, born in Grafton Regis in 1936, lived in the village for thirty years except when doing his National Service, and then moved to Alderton, two miles away. Maurice Allen, born at The Bank, Grafton Regis, in June 1920 and attended school in Grafton. Ron Allen, born in Silverstone in 1932 and brought to Grafton by his parents the following year to live in part of what is now Grove Cottage and later in Tudor Cottage. Ena and Ted Atkins, husband and wife. Ted's parents were known as Mr & Mrs At; the family came to Grafton Lodge in 1946.

Jane and Mahala Bagshaw, sisters born in the 1930s at Grafton Fields, which their father rented. Sarah and Becky Castle, daughters of Mont and Sheila Castle, were born in 1985 and 1990 respectively, and have lived all their lives in Grafton. John and Margaret Colgrove moved to Grafton to take over Paddocks Farm in 1956. David Edwards, Grafton-born, whose grandparents moved to the village in the 1920s.

Mrs Fountaine, the wife of an Alderton farmer, and the author of extensive diaries recording the 1950s and 1960s. Mrs Green of Roade, married to Percy Frank Green, who with his brother Dick worked at Grafton Fields in the 1930s when it was farmed by Gordon Bagshaw. Joan and John Harris, sister and brother, both born in Grafton Regis in the 1930s. The family lived in the School House until 1949/50. Sheila Jelley has undertaken extensive work on the Addington family and is a regular visitor to Grafton from Buckinghamshire.

Shirley Morris, née Allen, was born in Grafton in 1940, lived here until her marriage, and is a frequent visitor. Pete and Ron Plummer, brothers of Ken, to whom this book is dedicated. The Plummer family moved to Grafton from London during the Second World War. Robin Rogers, born at The Bank in 1941, where his mother, Jean Rogers, was also born. Joe Sargeant, owner of Grafton Lodge and discoverer of the Hermitage. Felicity Taylor, granddaughter of the Revd E.D. Annand, she spent holidays at The Cottage, which her father, a schoolmaster in Bath, rented from the Duke of Grafton. Joan Ward of Piddington, niece of Tom Elliott, farm manager at Grafton Lodge between the wars. Gilbert Wilson, came to Grafton in 1966, having married Joy, née Allen, three years earlier.

GRAFTON REGIS
MILLENNIUM COMMITTEE

Charles Reece, Chairman. Brought up in Grafton Lodge, Charles has lived in the village all his life and has become a great authority on all aspects of its history.

Charles FitzRoy, Editor of the historical chapters. Descended from the marriage of Edward IV and Elizabeth Woodville, and the Dukes of Grafton, Charles is currently writing a *Life of Charles II*.

Keith Harry, Editor of the final chapter. Keith has lived in the village since 1980, written widely on educational topics and is currently undertaking research for a history of the Open University.

Les Drake, Treasurer. Co-owner of the White Hart pub for the last three years, Les has become an enthusiastic supporter of Grafton's rich history.

Joy Wilson. Joy has lived in the parish of Grafton Regis all her life. A prime instigator of the book, her knowledge of the recent history of the village has been invaluable.

Sonia Baker. Sonia lives in one of the most historically interesting houses in the village, which dates back to the Middle Ages. Grafton Ward councillor, 1987–95.

Sarah Castle. Sarah represents the children of the village on the Committee; she has lived in Grafton Regis all her life.

ACKNOWLEDGEMENTS

We would like to thank all those who have contributed to the book. We are immensely grateful to Philip Riden, editor of the Northamptonshire Victoria County History, Tony Brown of the University of Leicester, Glenn Foard of Northamptonshire Heritage, Bob Kings of the Midlands Archaeological Research Society, and David Hall for sharing their profound knowledge of the village and its history, and for their generosity in contributing to the book. Dr Paul Bracewell of English Heritage, Dr Roger Lovatt of Peterhouse, Cambridge, Eric Christiansen of New College, Oxford, Paul Drewitt and Linda Allen have provided invaluable comments and advice on the text of the historical chapters.

As the book has developed, we have received very helpful advice from staff members of the Heritage Lottery Fund, the main sponsor of the project, in particular from Anne Jenkins and Amanda Newman. At the outset, John Myhill of South Northamptonshire Council, our second sponsor, gave us crucial guidance and support. The staff of our third sponsor, the White Hart public house in Grafton Regis, and in particular the Drake family, have been tireless in supporting and promoting the book, as well as providing the venue for our meetings.

The book could not have been completed without the help of all those who have contributed their memories of the village, which have been drawn upon in the final chapter, and we acknowledge their invaluable support. Many other people have also given their time and assistance to some aspect of work on the book, and our thanks are due to all of these, including Rachael Collins, Barry Glanville, Mike John, Rachel Smith. Stan Turner and Roy Welbourn, as well as to all of our respective families for their practical support and patience. Finally, our warm thanks go to all those people named in the list of subscribers.

Grafton Regis Millennium Committee

EDITORS' NOTE

The creation of a history of Grafton has required long and hard work and also a great deal of meticulous organisation. Here we must acknowledge the work of Charles Reece, the Committee Chairman, whose unstinting efforts and enthusiasm and commitment to the project have been so vital to the production of the book. Charles's own inspiration stems from Ken Plummer, who shortly before he died returned a letter from Ted Reece, Charles's father, thanking Ken for writing his 1959 history of Grafton. The letter records that all 500 copies were sold, at 2s. 6d. each. Ken in turn was inspired by the stories about Grafton which he heard as a child from Mrs At, his Sunday school teacher.

We also have to acknowledge the tireless work of Joy Wilson, who has not only contributed her extensive knowledge of the village to the project, but has also been responsible for collecting, in print and as audio conversations, the recollections of past and present villagers which form the foundation of the final chapter of the book.

Grafton Regis   *Charles FitzRoy*
May 2000   *Keith Harry*

FOREWORD

On the night of 23 December 1943 the four O'Donnell brothers and two friends, who had come from Ireland in search of agricultural work, had an extraordinary experience. In the early hours, asleep in their caravan in Park Close, they awoke to the sound of fighting. In the midst of a World War it was perhaps to be expected that conflict was much on men's minds. But this was a different kind of engagement, dominated by the noise of cannon firing, horses neighing and drums beating. The Irishmen lay petrified while the ghostly battle swirled around them. Next morning it proved almost impossible to resume work. They were even more reluctant when they discovered that their experience coincided with the 300th anniversary of the Siege of Grafton Manor in the Civil War.

The Irishmen's experiences, even allowing for the Guinness they may have consumed that night in the White Hart, shows how closely Grafton's history impinges on the present. Twenty years later, just a few yards from where they heard the ghostly sound of battle, the remains of a hermitage were uncovered, probably the site of Edward IV's marriage to Elizabeth Woodville. Beneath the fields surrounding the village lie coins, statuettes, buckles and spoons dating back to Roman times.

I am fascinated by the great moments of Grafton's history: the royal marriage, the fateful meeting of Henry VIII and Wolsey at the Manor, the drama of the Civil War siege, and the role that my ancestors, many of them buried in the church, played. My sons, however, born and brought up in Grafton, acquire a far more vivid record of the village's history by producing musket balls from their pockets when they return from playing Cavaliers and Roundheads in the fields. Now that they have seen the extent of Bob Kings's finds, they are hoping that their metal detector will unearth gold and silver beneath the ridge and furrow.

Much of the interest of this book lies in the story of the inhabitants up to the present day. Wartime reminiscences of the Home Guard or accounts of Percy Morton's shop spring vividly to life. Characters such as Chimp Richardson, who would regale the locals over a drink in the White Hart with tales of his life as a shepherd, form a vital link with the past. This book, with its sweep through two thousand years, shows how much of our country's history lies in the houses and fields of our own village, if we but take the trouble to search it out.

Charles FitzRoy

INTRODUCTION

The ancient village of Grafton Regis stands on a prominent spur overlooking the Tove valley about ten miles south of Northampton and four miles north-west of Stony Stratford. The parish is bounded on the north and east by the river Tove, which separates Grafton from Stoke Bruerne, Ashton, Hartwell and the Buckinghamshire parish of Hanslope; on the south by Yardley Gobion in the parish of Potterspury; and on the west by Paulerspury and Alderton. The land rises from the Tove valley in the east, which drops from about 250 ft above sea level at Twyford Bridge at the northern end of the parish to about 225 ft in the south, near the Yardley Gobion boundary, reaching a maximum height of some 340 ft on the higher ground to the south west. It is composed mostly of Oolitic limestone, overlaid towards the west and south-west by heavier clay.

The picturesque cluster of houses, based on a triangle of roads at the apex of the hill, extends from the church to the east side of the main Northampton–Stony Stratford road. Although it has shrunk since the Middle Ages, there are many reminders of the past, including ridge and furrow clearly visible in fields lying to the north of the village. The extensive woodland which once covered the surrounding area, and from which the name Grafton derives (a compilation of *grove* and *tun*), has now almost completely disappeared, with the exception of the 'Queen's Oak', just outside the parish boundary, now sadly a noble ruin, beneath which Edward IV is reputed to have met his beautiful wife Elizabeth Woodville. The parish is bisected by the main road which branches from Watling Street at Old Stratford to run north-north-east to Northampton and on to Nottingham. The road enters Grafton from the south by a crossing of the unnamed tributary of the Tove which here forms the parish boundary and leaves by Twyford Bridge, which carries the road over the Tove itself. The importance of this road, running from London to the Midlands, has ensured the village a prominent role in English history.

Despite its small size, Grafton Regis has enjoyed a rich and varied past. Mentioned in Domesday Book as *Grastone*, the village was the property of the abbey of Grestain in Normandy in the 12th and 13th centuries. The handsome Norman church dates from this period. The Woodvilles, who had lived in the village since the 12th century, acquired the manor in 1440. The vows exchanged in secret between Edward and

1

1 Grafton Regis and its neighbourhood in 1779, from Eyre and Jefferys's Map of Northamptonshire.

2 A postcard view of the Northampton–Stony Stratford road, looking south, *c*. 1910. This charming scene of a country lane is now the busy A508.

Elizabeth on May Day 1464 in Grafton give the village a role unique in English history.

The couple's daughter Elizabeth of York married Henry VII. Their son Henry VIII stayed at Grafton Manor many times, enjoying the hunting in the parks nearby. The King greatly enlarged the manor, extended the park to the west of the village, and added the epithet Regis to acknowledge the status of the village as the site of a royal palace. The royal residence was to be described a century later as 'the best and bravest seat in the kingdom, a seat fit for a prince and not a subject'. It was at Grafton that Henry conducted his last momentous interview with Wolsey and Cardinal Campeggio in 1529 before the King's divorce from Catherine of Aragon led to the historic break with the Church of Rome. Grafton played host to Elizabeth I and James I on several occasions, but the manor gradually fell into disrepair during the early 17th century.

The strategic importance of the village gave it a brief place on the national stage in the struggle to control the Midlands during the Civil War. A substantial Parliamentary force of 5,000 men under Major-General Skippon laid siege to Sir John Digby's Cavaliers in the Manor on 22 December 1643. The numerous musket balls which have been recently excavated around the village testify to the violence of the engagement. After a two-day assault, Digby capitulated on the afternoon of Christmas Eve before Prince Rupert could relieve the Royalist garrison. The Manor was almost completely destroyed during the siege.

After the Restoration the estate reverted to the Crown, from whom it passed to Charles II's natural son Henry FitzRoy, 1st Duke of Grafton. The arable and pasture land surrounding the village continued to be enclosed. Under the enlightened commissioners appointed by the 2nd Duke of Grafton the estate flourished, with the number of tenants continuing to rise throughout the 18th and 19th centuries. During this period most of the inhabitants were involved in agriculture although the village supported a number of inns as well as a shop and a smithy. Throughout the 18th century a manor court sat at Grafton. The 19th century saw increasing diversification in the village. A school was established in 1844. The agricultural backbone of the village came to an end with the break up of the Grafton estate in 1920, followed by the closure of the school fourteen years later.

Recently, there has been a revival in the village. Despite the ruthless destruction of the houses on the west side of the A508 to improve access to the M1 motorway, the nucleus of the village is still untouched and enjoys one of the most beautiful positions in south Northamptonshire. And yet, despite its extraordinary history, it is still much the same size as it was when mentioned in Domesday Book over nine hundred years ago.

EARLY HISTORY

By Anthony E. Brown

It seems probable that the Tove valley was progressively cleared and settled during the Neolithic and Bronze Ages. During the Iron Age and Roman period, despite some clearance and occupation, the presence of iron production on the clayland suggests that some woodland remained there at that time also. Under the Roman occupation, Watling Street, running from London to Chester and one of the most important roads in England, now the A5, lay a few miles west of the village, and numerous villas were laid out in the vicinity. During the unsettled times which followed the Roman withdrawal, much of the the boulder clayland ceased to be farmed and reverted to woodland.

A prehistoric site, 20 m. in diameter, with a dark area and many burnt pebbles, lies at National Grid reference SP 7481 4537, west of Grafton Fields Farm. It probably represents a communal cooking area dating to about 2500 BC. Late Iron Age pottery sherds (c. 50 BC) are scattered over an area of dark soil just west of the A508, at SP 7545 4635. South of Grafton Lodge a large Roman site, most likely the remains of a farmstead, has produced sherds, building stone and black soil spread over a low uneven area at SP 7500 4620. More Roman sherds (3rd-century AD) and building stone lie at SP 7552 4580, in an area about 50 m. diameter. As well as the medieval and earlier remains within the confines of the village described below, to the west of the A508 are two medieval fishponds made by building dams across the stream that flows there (SP 7545 4635).

The Village Plan and its Evolution

The archaeological work in Grafton Parish just described provides evidence for human activity in the area from the Neolithic period onwards. This section carries the story forward by looking in detail at the site of the village itself. It is hoped that the following account will show that there is reasonable evidence for human occupation on the site of the village of Grafton Regis from at least the late Iron Age (say the first millennium BC) right up to the present day. This evidence consists of the

5

conclusions to be drawn from the earthworks which used to exist in grassland in the fields to the south of the church and which still do in fields in other parts of the village; the results of the systematic field-walking of the now largely ploughed-out earthworks in the fields opposite the church; the study of various aerial photographs; and work with Ordnance Survey maps of various dates and an estate survey of 1725 in the Northamptonshire Record Office.

Earthworks

We can begin by looking at the plan of the earthworks (Fig. 3). They fall into a number of parts.

(i) Immediately to the north of the more northerly of the pair of roads which run from the A508 is a substantial bank (a) up to 10 m. wide and in places 0.5 m. high showing as a light mark on the RAF vertical air photographs taken in 1947 and probably representing the northern wall of an enclosed warren marked here on the map of 1725. The southern wall of the warren, at (b), is still in existence.

(ii) In the triangular area between the two roads is a series of house platforms (c-d), some battered, and behind them the irregular earthworks of former limestone quarrying (e). No houses were shown at (c) on the early map and only one at (d), apparently a cottage right at the apex of the triangle of land.

(iii) Opposite the church was a small paddock, grass when it was surveyed in 1983 but later ploughed up, containing the earthworks of a boundary ditch, or possibly a path, 10 m. wide (g). This corresponded with a hedge on the early map. North of the boundary the map shows three smallish buildings; their sites were marked by a series of irregular scarps at (h).

(iv) The field to the south of the grass paddock had been ploughed up by the time the earthworks came to be surveyed. The somewhat levelled remains consist, at (i) and (j), of a low scarp delimiting the southern part of what could have been a large sub-rectangular enclosure. The survey showed quite clearly that at (j) this had been over ploughed with ridge and furrow; this effect is not quite so apparent on some air photographs of the area taken when the field was under grass, which show the line of the scarp at (j) being used as the junction between a pair of furlongs; the effect of the ploughing up has been to remove the earthworks of the headlands to reveal the original, longer, plough ridges running through below them. At (k) and (l) are further limestone quarries while at (m) a hollow-way, with house platforms and property boundaries on either

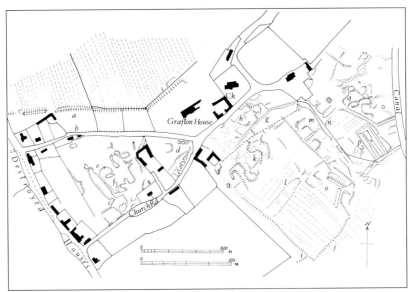

3 Medieval and earlier earthworks at Grafton Regis.

side of it and a hedge along its length, runs southwards, turning abruptly to the east after 180 m.; a second hollow-way left it at (n). At (o) is a pair of mounds, both 40 m. long and 10 m. wide, shown on aerial photographs as formerly existing within an irregular ditched enclosure, now largely ploughed out, the whole probably a rabbit warren. In the grass field opposite at (p) is a set of very regular and shallow fishponds fed by a stream following the line of the hollow-way (m). Both warren and ponds in part overlie the earlier settlement remains along the hollow-way. On the early map the two modern fields then formed a single large one called Old Park, the name suggesting an amenity area associated with the medieval Grafton House, which lay directly opposite on the site of the present one. They contained ponds in which Henry VIII may have fished. The adjective 'old' might suggest that the earthwork warren here had perhaps been replaced by the walled one to the northwest by the time the map had been made.

(v) At (q) is a pair of embanked ponds and an area of disturbed ground connected with the natural drainage at this point: a number of streams emerge at the junction of the Upper Lias clay and the limestones above and the whole area is marshy and poorly drained. Although these ponds appear on the 1947 RAF vertical air photographs they were not there in the early years of this century, on the evidence of the Ordnance Survey 25-inch maps.

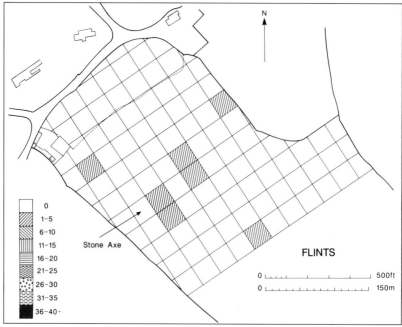

4 Distribution of flints found during fieldwalking at Grafton Regis.

Fieldwalking

The two fields opposite the church were amalgamated and ploughed up
in 1984. They were divided up into 30 m. squares and systematically
walked to record archaeological material (see Figs. 4–10). The results
were as follows:

(i) A thin scatter of prehistoric flint flakes, and also the butt end of a
Neolithic polished stone axe, belonging to Group 6 (from Great Langdale
in the Lake District);

(ii) A scatter of Iron Age pottery, including Belgic forms, and a
bronze coin of Cunobelin (King of the Catavellani in the early part of the
first century AD) concentrated around (i) and (l).

(iii) Roman pottery, of 2nd- to 4th-century types, with the same
general concentration;

(iv) Early to mid Anglo-Saxon pottery ranging from the 5th to 9th
centuries, again concentrated in the same areas.

(v) A thin scatter of 10th- and 11th-century late Saxon black shelly
ware, with no obvious concentration.

(vi) Abundant medieval pottery: shelly wares, sandy Potterspury wares
and dark sandy pieces, including vessels made at Brickhill in

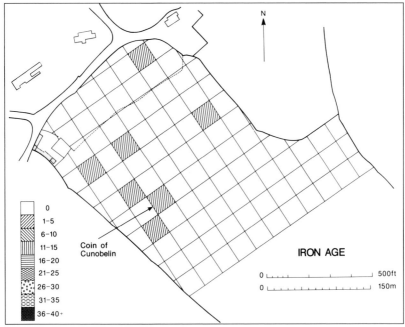

5 Distribution of Iron Age finds.

Buckinghamshire, mainly of the 12th to 15th centuries. This came in bulk from the line of battered settlement remains to the west of the hollow-way (m), from (h), and also from the area of the Iron Age-Roman and early to mid Saxon scatter. The pottery from (m), together with the earthworks, suggests an early medieval expansion of settlement along the track, but also suggests that contraction had taken place sometime in the 14th and 15th centuries. Fragmentary remains of houses on both sides of the hollow-way, along with pits and ditches, were found here during pipeline laying in 1979; the associated pottery covered the span 1100–1500, with a single unstratified piece of Northampton ware of 850–1100.

(vii) A general scatter of 17th- and 18th-century pottery around (h), where the cottages were marked on the map of 1725.

General Observations

The concentration of Iron Age to mid Saxon pottery around (i) and (l) is of great interest; of course field walking cannot prove continuous occupation, but it can suggest it. Also, this occupation is contained

Grafton Regis

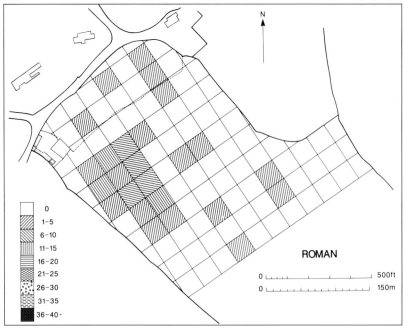

6 Distribution of Roman finds.

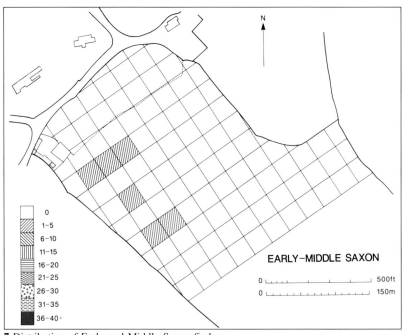

7 Distribution of Early and Middle Saxon finds.

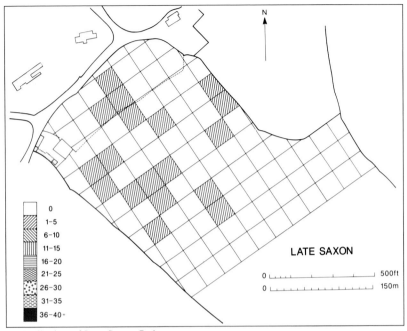

8 Distribution of Late Saxon finds.

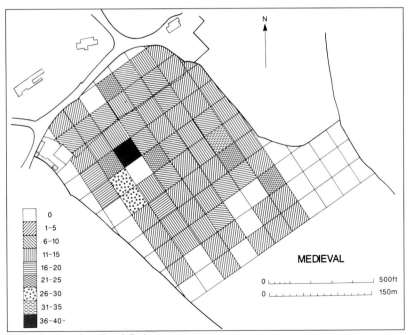

9 Distribution of medieval finds.

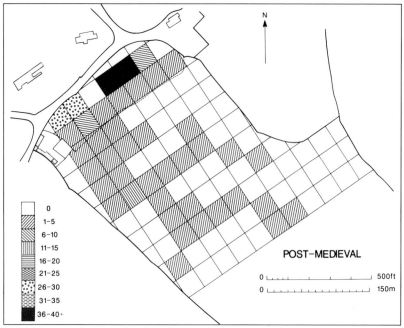

10 Distribution of post-medieval finds.

within what could have been a sub-rectangular enclosure, of uncertain
but relatively early date on the evidence of its relationship with the ridge
and furrow. The northern boundary was probably the ditch or track (g);
the eastern boundary the hollow-way (m) rather than the scarp representing the rearward boundary of the properties set out along the western
side of the track in the 12th century. So the possibility exists here of the
identification of an early earthwork feature in a village context. The
existence of this early site, on a favoured south-facing slope, may have
been an important factor in determining the plan of the village. The
houses of the present village and the earthworks of former house sites
could well represent the expansion of settlement along a series of roads
and tracks, which converge upon it. The pair of roads coming in from
the west and forming a triangle represent the general line of routes from
Paulerspury and Potterspury; the roads and tracks running off to the east,
(m) included, went across the River Tove to various elements in the
pattern of dispersed settlement in the parishes of Hartwell and Hanslope.
The narrow strip north-west of (i), between (i) and the hedge, seems to
have acted as a field road for the ridge and furrow furlongs as far as the
parish boundary, 800 m. to the south-east.

The sparseness of the late Saxon pottery may indicate that this particular site came to an end in that period, but the evidence is inconclusive; there is plenty of medieval pottery from the 12th century onwards, in the same general area as the earlier material. It is not beyond the bounds of possibility that the single farm, with one bordar with one plough, which is all that Domesday records for Grafton in 1086, lay here.

The church was presumably in existence *c.* 1100 since it is mentioned in the confirmation charter of Richard I's reign as having been granted along with the estate to the Norman abbey of Grestain by William Count of Mortain. The first reference to a manor house comes in 1205, when a building with a chief court is referred to in an inquisition. These features would represent a shift in the focus of the settlement to higher ground under the earls of Mortain and the Woodvilles, sub-tenants of the Norman abbey. The area around (h) looks like a green, subsequently partially encroached upon: perhaps the location of the market and fair granted to Earl Rivers *c.* 1467. To what extent the settlement earthworks in the area of the Old Park represent a contraction of settlement due to economic forces in the late medieval period, or whether any physical removal of houses took place, is unknown. The end result was to produce a large enclosure opposite the manor house fitted up to further the pleasurable and sporting activities for which Grafton became well known at the highest social level in the 15th and later 16th centuries, which will be described later in this book.

THE MIDDLE AGES

The amount of archaeological material in and around the village testifies to its importance in the Middle Ages and to the role Grafton assumed on the national stage in the 15th century.

The Manor

In 1066 the manor of Grafton was held freely by the Saxon Godwin, who also had estates nearby at Cosgrove and Furtho. After the battle of Hastings, the victorious Norman knights were given vast land holdings throughout England. Grafton was given to Robert Count of Mortain, half-brother of William the Conqueror, whose sub-tenant William held four-fifths of one hide, as recorded in Domesday Book in 1086. The Normans retained strong links with their native Normandy. Sometime between 1086 and 1106 (when his estates were forfeit by rebellion), Robert's son and successor Count William gave to the abbot and convent of Nôtre-Dame de Grestain, a Benedictine house near the mouth of the Seine founded by William's grandfather in 1040, all that he possessed in Grafton, together with the church there. The abbot of Grestain thus appears as the tenant of Grafton in the early 12th-century survey of Northamptonshire.

Grestain continued to hold Grafton until the middle of the 14th century, at which time there were seven free tenants and 15 other tenants of the manor, the number later rising to 31 tenants. Most of the abbey's dealings with the village refer to disputes over ownership, the abbot's gift of six oaks to Grafton in 1245 being a rare exception. The abbey was generally successful in resisting the claims of various parties, including that of Walter de Wideville, lord of Grafton (the first mention of the famous name of Woodville which was to form such a central part of Grafton's history).

However, its absentee role became more complicated at the beginning of the Hundred Years' War between England and France. The patron of Grestain, Jehan de Melun, Sire de Tancarville, was captured at the battle of Crécy in 1348, the great victory won by Edward III's son the Black Prince, who gained his spurs on the field of battle. This was also the year of the Black Death, and with the twin scourges of war and the plague devastating the north of France, the abbot of Grestain was hard pressed to raise a ransom for his patron. He decided to dispose of the abbey's holding at Grafton to a merchant named Tidemann de Lymbergh. Tidemann appears to have been acting simply as a middleman: in 1350 he secured a licence to grant the former Grestain estates to any Englishman he chose, to be held of the king by the service of one knight's fee, and four years later sold his holding at Grafton to Sir Michael de la Pole, a wealthy Hull merchant, for the remainder of the term of a thousand years. Grafton, together with some of the other former Grestain manors which had passed through Tidemann de Lymbergh's hands, remained in the possession of the de la Pole family for the next three generations.

Michael de la Pole had one of the most spectacular careers in late medieval England. In 1385 he was created Earl of Suffolk and Chancellor of England, but the following year he was impeached and convicted by Parliament, with many of his lands forfeit. The proceedings against him were declared void in August 1387 but, fearing for his life, in December that year he fled the realm. In his absence he was found guilty by Parliament in February 1388 of high treason, and all his honours forfeit. He died at Paris in 1389. Nevertheless, the manor remained in the possession of the de la Pole family for a further fifty years. In 1440 it passed to Richard Wideville and his wife Jacquetta (see p. 25). From about this date the mansion can legitimately be called a 'manor house' as the home of the Wideville family, during which time the village was known as Grafton Wideville. A measure of Grafton's increasing importance during this period can be gauged from the grant made by Earl Rivers (as Richard Wideville had become) in 1465 of a weekly market at his manor of Grafton to be held every Thursday, and two annual fairs, on the feasts of St Mary Magdalen and SS. Simon and Jude.

Before the advent of the Woodvilles, as they came to be called, Grafton played a peripheral role in English history. Nevertheless, standing on one of the main roads from the capital to the north, it witnessed many stirring events, including the funeral cortege of Queen Eleanor of Castile, wife of Edward I. The great medieval King, conqueror of Wales and 'Hammer of the Scots', was devastated by the death of his beloved wife at Harby in Nottinghamshire on 4 December 1290. Eleanor had been his constant companion for many years, and had even accompanied her husband on the Crusades, where she is supposed to have sucked poison from his wound. The King commanded that her body be brought to London for burial in Westminster Abbey (although her heart and entrails were buried separately in Lincoln), and that crosses be erected wherever her body rested for the night, surmounted by statues of the Queen, hair loose, a sceptre in her right hand. On 9 December the procession wound its way slowly past the village of Grafton, *en route* from Northampton, where Eleanor's Cross still stands, to Stony Stratford. The final landmark at Charing Cross remains one of the most evocative sites in London.

The Church

The dominant buildings in Grafton during the Middle Ages were the Norman church of St Mary the Virgin, begun in the 12th century, and the manor house. It is not clear whether anything of the 12th-century building survives, as the church appears to have been built mainly in the Decorated style (*c.* 1290–*c.* 1350), though the north arcade dates from the early 13th century and the tower from the 15th century. The exterior of this tower has a polygonal turret staircase. The building is constructed of coursed, squared limestone, with a slate roof over the nave and a lead one over the chancel, tower and porch. This porch, with its two stone benches, is the main entrance to the church and was formerly a meeting-place for the villagers, both socially and for business. The interior was substantially restored in the 19th century (see p. 88).

The four bays of the north arcade contain circular piers and abaci, and hood-moulds with small zigzags. There are a number of interesting features: the lack of a corresponding aisle on the south side of the nave is unusual. Also, there is no clerestory and the nave is therefore directly lit from the south side apart from two small windows at the east end which may have been intended to cast light on the rood screen. The remains of the screen consist of a damaged panel of *The Passion of Christ* hanging over the south side of the chancel. Beneath it there is an interesting sedilia (a seat for priests) and a piscina (a basin for washing communion vessels), with a priest's doorway between, all ogee-arched. The east window is in the more elaborate Perpendicular style (*c.* 1340–*c.* 1530). The font at the west end of the nave is Norman. Beyond it stands the tower, built by Sir John Woodville, with its five bells, one inscribed 'Ave Maria Gratia Plena' ('Hail Mary full of Grace'), another 'In Multis Annis resonet Campana Johannis' ('For many years may the bell John sound out'). Two more are dated 1625 and inscribed 'God Save the King'.

The fine early 15th-century tomb of Sir John Woodville, with its seven ogee-headed panels, lies in the north aisle of the church, having been moved from the north side of the chancel where the organ now stands. In Bridges's words: 'On the sides of this monument were shields of brass hung upon hooks'. Baker, in his *History of Northamptonshire*,

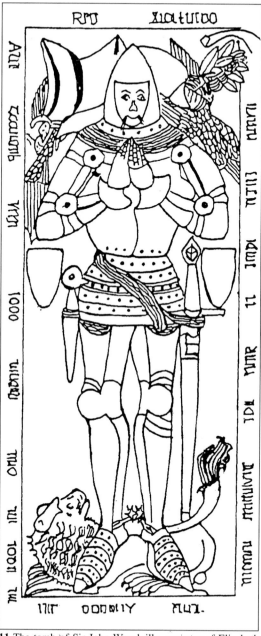

11 The tomb of Sir John Woodville, ancestor of Elizabeth Woodville, Queen of England, in the north aisle of Grafton Regis church. He built the tower of the church.

describes the figure: 'On the alabaster slab is engraved a remarkably fine full-sized figure of Sir John Wydeville in a suit of plate armour, with his hands elevated and conjoined'. He continues with an intricate description of the armour: 'To his conical basinet studded across the forehead is attached a gorget of plate, edged with mail, and the upper part studded; circular pallettes in front of his armpits and elbows; gauntlets cuffed and jointed; tassettes of overlapping plates edged with mail, and each lamina studded; jointed sollerets with pointed toes, and rowelled spurs. At his right side is an anelace or dagger with no apparent fastening, and at his left, a long sword suspended from a diagonally placed belt buckled in front. He has moustachios but no beard. His head rests upon an unusually large tilting helmet crested with a bird in a tree, and is supported on each side by a winged cherub. His feet are placed on a lion regardant'. The inscription on the tomb reads: 'John Wydville who by God's good grace built the Bell Tower, now at its foot, lies beneath this stone. Be gracious, O God, and by thy grace afford him thine aid: O God, do thou protect thyself, and thy Mother also'. The adjacent tomb, also in the Gothic style, reputed by hearsay to be of a royalist killed during the siege of 1643, is much more likely to be of another member of the Woodville family. The later monuments to the FitzRoy family and the 19th-century stained glass are mentioned later (pp. 87–8).

The Village

A substantial complex of buildings stood immediately to the west of the church in the Middle Ages. As well as the church and manor house, most of the remaining settlement of the parish stood on one of the two lanes running from the church to the main road, or on the main road itself. The row of tenements facing south on the present Church Lane may possibly have been laid out over former open-field furlongs, at least at its western end. Originally the road may have lain to the north of Church Lane, giving a nearly straight frontage with the manor and the church, which lay at the eastern end of the row. Only later was this probably encroached upon with the establishment of the town house and gardens.

On the south side of Church Lane was a row of shallow tenements divided by a small green, with a road running around their southern side. Another road ran at right angles to Church Lane in the medieval period. Although only the Old Rectory remains at the northern end of this road, close to its junction with Church Lane, there are earthworks of tenements on both sides of it, indicating medieval occupation probably abandoned in the 14th or 15th centuries. This may have been caused by the shift in the axis of the village towards the main road, with its commercial potential. This would explain the presence of the King's Arms and also perhaps the forge on the west side of the road. The two buildings would appear to have been established as encroachments onto the waste, infilling ground between the park pale and the highway.

There is some confusion over the medieval road system in Grafton, particularly the main road from Northampton to Old Stratford. The secondary nature of this road is evident from the way in which it runs straight across the township, avoiding the original village. It has the appearance, lying at the western edge of the village and cutting across an earlier road pattern, of a major new road. However, the way in which it follows the northern third of the boundary which divides Grafton from Alderton implies either a pre-Conquest origin for the road or a medieval reorganisation of the field systems of the two villages.

The Hermitage

A hermit established himself a short distance west of the main road, apparently towards the end of the 12th century. He was probably living under the Augustinian rule and may have moved to Grafton from St James's Abbey in Northampton. The site of the hermitage may have been determined by the road running from Grafton to Alderton, now a public footpath, which was closed when the park was extended in the 16th century. By 1256, or a little before, the house had grown into a small religious community and continued to prosper during the following century. The post of master of the hermitage was obviously a prestigious one, since the Woodvilles (to avoid confusion we have used this spelling despite numerous alternatives such as Wideville, Widvile, Wivill, Wyvill and Wydeville) were obliged to defend their position as patron at the King's court in Westminster from rival claimants. They were successful, and William of Radford in 1340 and Simon of Olney in 1349 were both their appointments. In the wake of the Black Death in 1348, however, the fortune of the building declined. The appointment of Walter Childe, 'priest of the chantry of the hermitage of St Michael at Grafton', in 1370 is the last record we have. The hermitage became a perpetual chantry belonging to the Woodville family, one of whom (Thomas Woodville, who died in 1435) tried unsuccessfully to persuade St James's to resume responsibility for the house, with the request that they maintain five poor men and a keeper. At some point in Edward IV's reign, possibly because they were unhappy at the abbey's failure to act, the Woodvilles took over the chantry again and undertook a major reconstruction of the building, which they may have used as a private chapel in this period. After the Woodvilles' fall from power the house probably again fell into decay and may have been suppressed by St James's well before the abbey itself was dissolved in 1538.

The site was extensively excavated in 1964–5 when a pillared cloister, measuring some 34 ft by 35 ft internally, was found, flanked by a chapel (48 ft by 15 ft) and several other buildings, some of two storeys. Beyond lay a dovecote, what may have been a hospital, and an industrial complex, including a malt kiln and an emplacement for a brewer's vat. During the 15th-century rebuilding the cloister was sealed off and the chapel refloored with tiles decorated with the arms of Woodville and the

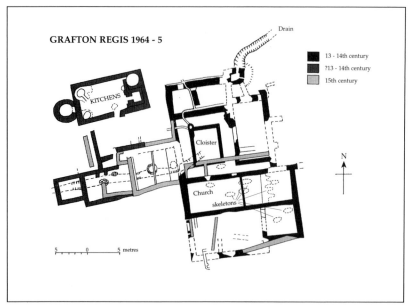

12 The Hermitage at Grafton Regis, as excavated in 1964–5. Probably the site of Elizabeth Woodville's secret marriage to Edward IV on May Day 1464.

house of York, a feature that has led to the suggestion that the chapel may have been the scene of the marriage between Edward IV and Elizabeth Woodville in 1464. After the chantry was suppressed, the buildings were demolished and the site later absorbed into the park which in the 16th century came to occupy much of the south-western corner of the parish.

The Medieval Open Fields

Fig. 13 shows the ridge and furrow of Grafton parish. This represents the open fields of the medieval village. In the Middle Ages a farm, called a yardland, consisted of about 25 acres of land lying scattered in strips throughout a township, no two strips lying together. The long narrow parcels were called lands by those who worked them and often have dimensions of about 7 m. by 200 m. Furrows were aligned down hill, across the contours, to give natural surface drainage. Groups of lands lying parallel to each other were called furlongs, and were identified by names. Most of the available ground in a parish was ploughed and only river meadows liable to flooding, wet areas along the side of brooks, and areas with steep and rough ground were left unploughed.

Ridges were created by ploughing clockwise, beginning in the middle and going round and round until the outside was reached. To prevent furrows cutting deeply into infertile subsoil, an anti-clockwise ploughing motion was adopted in the fallow season to take some of the soil back and maintain a low ridge. The purpose of a ridging was to obtain a well drained seed-bed and the furrow acted as a drain as well as providing a clear demarcation between lands.

For the purposes of cropping, furlongs were grouped together in large open, unhedged areas called fields. Typically there would be three fields in a township, two of which would be cropped, leaving the other one fallow; each became fallow in turn in succeeding years, so forming an arrangement known as the three-field system. It is for this reason that a single holding had to be scattered uniformly throughout the arable lands; if it was not then all or most of the land belonging to a particular farm might lie in the fallow field in one year and there would be no produce for the farmer to live on. The fallow field, although producing no crop, was used as rough grazing for the village animals because of the shortage of meadow land. It was essential to have a large block of land to keep the common herd together and prevent it wandering over the cultivated area.

The degree of surviving ridging varies according to the soil type (clay ground being well developed), but the main influence is the date of enclosure, since there is a general trend that ridging gets steeper with time. In old enclosure, ridge and furrow has a low profile compared to the sharp profile of ridges ploughed until the 18th and 19th centuries. All that now remain at Grafton have rather a low profile because of the early date of enclosure. The ends of most lands are curved, so that the whole land took the shape of a very elongated, mirror-image of an **S**. This seems to have developed over the years, resulting from a tendency first to draw out to the left when performing a turning circle to the right.

As well as moving soil towards the centre of the land, the action of the plough moved small quantities in the direction of motion, towards the ends. This soil was deposited when the plough was lifted out of the ground to turn. Over the years small heaps, called 'heads', formed at each end. These movements of soil fossilised the physical pattern of the open fields into the landscape, leaving earthwork remains that allow furlongs to be mapped by archaeological fieldwork. When a ridged grassy field is ploughed flat, the soil piled up at the end of the lands does not become much flattened by modern ploughing, but gets merged with the heads of the neighbouring lands, the whole series forming a long, smooth bank lying along the edge of a furlong. So wherever a group of lands, a furlong, merged with another one, either orientated in the same

Grafton Furlong Names in 1725

See map opposite

Sties Field		acres
1	Stieslane furlong	8
2	Sties furlong	3
3	Church lays	1
4	Wellspring furlong	9
5	Wellspring lays	3
6	Hill furlong	4
7	Iron furlong	8
8	Dearleap furlong	4
9	Middle furlong	17
10	Brook furlong	8
11	Gogmoor lays	4
12	Gogmoor lays	9
13	Stone bridge lays	3
14	Stone Bridge corner	6
15	Furlong to Gogmoore lays	10
16	Nether furlong	19

Grafton Upper Common Field		acres
1	Low furlong	16
2	Middle furlong	12
3	Hill furlong	5
4	Upper furlong	5

Grafton Fen Common Field		
1	Upper furlong	13
2	Yardly hedge furlong	10
3	Furlong to mill gap	3
4	Mill gap lays	2
5	Lower furlong	15
6	Foard leys	4
7	Lot meadow	7

Grafton Bancroft Common Field		
1	Yardly hedge furlong	13
2	Plainslade lays	1
3	Plain furlong	7
4	Fen hedge butts furlong	2
5	Fen hedge side furlong	2
6	Butts to Fen Hedge	2
7	Lord Duke's acre	1
8	Hill furlong	4
9	[no name]	1
10	Hole furlong	3
11	Glebe piece	1
12	Highway furlong	14
13	Fen gap furlong	9
14	Five lays	1

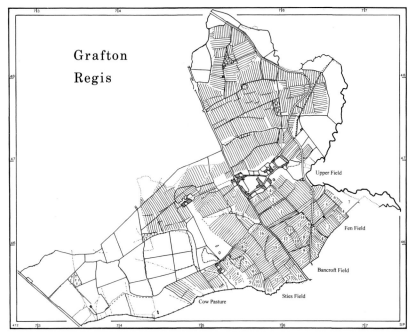

13 The open fields. Thick lines are modern field boundaries; furlong boundaries (thin lines at right angles to the strips) were recorded by field survey in 1998.

direction, or at right angles, a bank of soil will survive. The positions of ridges are visible for some time as light and dark soil marks. Lines of light colour derive from subsoil exposed in the old ridges and the dark lines are caused by humus lying buried in the furrows.

A survey of furlong boundary soil banks in an entire township allows a map of the furlongs to be made, even if there are no old grass fields of ridge and furrow left at all. The results can be supplemented by reference to aerial photographs, especially those taken in the late 1940s by the RAF. A set taken on 15 April 1947 covers the centre and west of the county.

Studies elsewhere have shown that ridge and furrow was commonly laid out in the 9th century. At Grafton the parish fields were grouped into three by 1315, called the North Field, East Field and South Field. The first presumably lay to the north of the village between the main road (which here forms the boundary with Alderton) and the river; the second to the south-east, again between the main road and the Tove; and the third to the south-west, beyond the main road.

The Park and Woodland

There was evidently a park adjoining the manor to the south-east in the Middle Ages, since the name 'Old Park' survived for the large field across the road from the house until modern times. This was presumably disparked in Henry VIII's time, when a much larger park was created to the west of the main road.

To the west of the village there was a medieval park, visible as a curved kidney shape in the field pattern, with an irregular western end that may be a medieval extension. Parks were enclosed with earthen ramparts to exclude animals and poachers, and to keep deer in. Grafton Park boundary is preserved as a bank with a slight external ditch on the north-west at SP 7415 4592 for a length of 250 m. More remains lie at the east, at SP 7500 4573. The finest rampart of the park complex lies in the little wood now called Grafton Park, at SP 7345 4560, where a length of 130 m. survives as a mound 1.5 m. high and 7 m. wide, with slight ditches on both sides. Parks had within them woods or coppices and open spaces of pasture called lawns. The coppices acted as a source of underwood and timber and as cover for deer. The lawns yielded hay and grazing. During hunting, deer were chased out of the coppices and pursued over the lawns. The original park lodge site was probably located north of the ruins of the present Grafton Cottage Farm at SP 7420 4584 (a house is marked there in 1721).

The north-western extremity of Grafton parish extended to within a short distance of Alderton village: a small portion of land here formed part of Alderton common fields prior to enclosure and was let thereafter with one of the Alderton farms. This, together with the way in which until 1883 the parish of Alderton included an area of former common meadow which geographically lay wholly within Grafton, possibly suggests that in the early Middle Ages the two formed a single estate. The case for this is perhaps supported by the fact that both parishes are bounded on the north and south by the same natural feature, i.e. the Tove to the north and an unnamed east-flowing tributary to the south.

EDWARD IV

AND ELIZABETH WOODVILLE

The most important family in Grafton in the later Middle Ages were the Woodvilles, who came to play such a vital role in English history. There is a record of a Woodville in Grafton as early as the late 12th century, when a William de Woodville paid a rent of 25s. yearly to the abbot of Grestain. Woodville was probably unhappy to pay this rent to an absentee landlord, and in 1235, in a complex legal case heard in the court of the the hundred of Cleley (a group of thirteen parishes in the south of the county), his son Walter de Woodville unsuccessfully challenged the abbot's title to the lordship of Grafton. Although the case failed, the family continued to rise in importance. By 1297 John de Woodville held lands valued at £20 yearly and was required to perform military service in person overseas under Edward I. His son, another John de Woodville, claimed privileges from Cleley hundred in 1329. John's son Richard served as high sheriff eight times during the reign of Edward III, and sat in seven Parliaments. His son Sir John is buried in the church (see p. 17).

John's grandson Thomas owned a substantial estate in Grafton and its neighbouring parishes. On his death in 1435, his half-brother Richard inherited, and it was his son, also confusingly called Richard, who acquired the manor from William de la Pole, 4th Earl of Suffolk, in June 1440. The elder Richard had served under Henry V and was appointed seneschal of Normandy. His son Richard was a leading supporter of Henry VI and offered his sovereign a force of one hundred men at arms and three hundred archers to fight in France. This offer was accepted, and Richard served with distinction in the Hundred Years' War under the leading English generals Talbot and Henry V's brother the Duke of Bedford. He was knighted at Leicester and Shakespeare records in *Henry VI, Part 1*, 'Woodville, Lieutenant of the Tower', an ironic post in view of the fate of his two grandsons.

On Bedford's death, Sir Richard Woodville married the duke's widow Jacquetta, daughter of the Duke of Luxembourg, with unseemly haste, probably in 1436. The couple were both noted for their striking looks and were reputed to be the handsomest couple in England. For neglecting to ask permission from the King, Jacquetta was fined £1,000, a vast sum in those days. Interestingly, the House of Tudor descends from a similar misalliance since, at much the same date, Henry V's widow Katherine, a Princess of France, remarried the humble Owen Tudor, Henry VII's grandfather.

The Woodvilles soon returned to royal favour, however, partly because of the close relationship between Jacquetta and Queen Margaret of Anjou, wife of Henry VI; both women were French princesses in a foreign land. The couple's eldest child Elizabeth, the first of five sons and seven daughters, was born in 1437, probably at Grafton. She spent her early years in France, where she is very likely to have known the young Edward of York, born in Rouen in 1442. In 1448 Elizabeth's father was created Baron Rivers 'for his valour, integrity and great services', and was given free warren of all his lands in Northamptonshire in 1457. Henry further rewarded Woodville by making him a Knight of the Garter and seneschal of Aquitaine at the head of 300 spearmen and 2,700 bowmen. Woodville's wife Jacquetta was similarly favoured by Margaret of Anjou, who gave her valuable jewels and appointed her little daughter maid of honour.

When the Wars of the Roses broke out in 1455 between supporters of Henry VI and the House of Lancaster on one side, and supporters of the Duke of York on the other, both men claiming descent from Edward III, the Woodvilles were staunch adherents of Henry VI and the Red Rose. By now Elizabeth was one of four ladies of the Queen's bedchamber. By 1456 she had married Sir John Grey of Groby, another loyal follower of Henry VI. Five years later, on 17 February 1461, Grey was killed at the second battle of St Albans, leading the last charge of the Lancastrians on the Yorkist line. His widow with her two young sons almost certainly returned to live with her parents at Grafton.

At this date, the leader of the Yorkist faction was the 19-year-old Edward, Duke of York. With his striking red-gold hair, which his Tudor descendants were to inherit, he stood 6 feet 3 inches high, a giant among his contemporaries. Edward was a born leader and had already proved himself on the field of battle. His open-hearted manner had won him widespread popularity and he was renowned for his grace and strength, and his prowess as a swordsman and dancer. Philip de Commynes, a contemporary Burgundian chronicler, describes him as 'a man of goodly personages, of stature high, and exceeding all other in countenance, well favoured and comely, of eyes quick and pleasant, broad-breasted and well set'. Already he had acquired a reputation as a womaniser; the Croyland Chronicle comments on how he was 'fond of boon-companionships, vanities, debaucheries, extravagance and sensual enjoyments'.

14 A painting of the Queen's Oak, near Grafton Regis. Beneath this venerable tree Edward IV is reputed to have met and fallen in love with Elizabeth Woodville in 1461.

Following his victory over the Lancastrians at Mortimer's Cross on 2 February 1461, and with the help of his cousin Richard Neville, Earl of Warwick, the greatest nobleman in the land, fresh from his victory at the battle of St Albans, Edward claimed the thone and was crowned in Westminster Abbey on 4 March. There were now two Kings in England. It was inevitable that they would clash. Edward marched north and on Palm Sunday, in a snowstorm, won a hard-fought victory at Towton in Yorkshire, one of the bloodiest battles of the Middle Ages. After spending Easter in the city of York, the triumphant general slowly made his way south.

It was beneath the Queen's Oak while hunting in Whittlewood Forest that the King is reputed to have met Elizabeth Woodville. The only sources for this encounter are the later Tudor chroniclers Edward Hall and Sir Thomas More, although the Queen's Oak, a venerable tree still standing between Grafton Regis and Watling Street, is always said to be the site of their first meeting. Elizabeth is supposed to have pleaded with the King to restore her family's lands at Grafton. Edward was smitten by the sight of this beautiful damsel in distress. There is some evidence to support this romantic story. When the King left Stony Stratford two days later, he had 'pardoned and remitted and forgiven unto Richard Woodville, Lord Rivers, all manners of offences and trespasses done against us', though this may have been due to overtures made by Rivers himself after Towton. The King further instructed his Treasurer to pay Elizabeth's mother Jacquetta the annual amount of her dowry.

Hall, in his Chronicle, gives a vivid if fanciful account of the fateful meeting: 'For, during the time that the Earl of Warwick was thus in France concluding a marriage for King Edward, the King, being hunting in the forest of Wychwood beside Stony Stratford, came for his recreation to the Manor of Grafton, where the Duchess of Bedford sojourned, then being wife of Sir Richard Woodville, Lord Rivers, on whom was attending a daughter of hers called Dame Elizabeth Gray, widow of Sir John Gray, Knight, slain at the last battle of St Albans, by the power of King Edward. This widow having a suit to the King … found such grace in the King's eyes that he not only favoured her suit, but much more fantasied her person … For she was a woman … of such beauty and favour with her sober demeanour, lovely looking and feminine smiling (neither too wanton nor too humble)'.

Whatever the truth of the purported meeting, at some point in the early 1460s Edward fell in love with Elizabeth. Contemporary and later sources agree that Elizabeth utterly refused to compromise her chastity, declaring: 'she knew herself unworthy to be a queen, but valued her honour more than to be a concubine'. Antonio Cornazzano, reporting back to the ruling Sforzas in Milan, claimed that she was compelled to defend herself with a dagger against the advances of the King. We have no actual accounts of the couple meeting during this period, but in July 1463 Edward spent three weeks in Northampton, and he was back again in the following January. By the spring of 1464 he had determined to make Elizabeth his wife.

This decision was fraught with danger. By taking an English wife, the first monarch to do so since Henry I, and one whose paternal ancestry was far from grand, Edward risked alienating the nobility. In addition, the Woodville support for the Red Rose was bound to antagonise the

King's Yorkist supporters. Moreover, his cousin Richard Neville, Earl of Warwick, to whom, more than any other man, Edward owed his crown, was in the process of negotiating an alliance with France based on a marriage between the King and the King Louis XI of France's sister-in-law Bona of Savoy.

Following the Garter service at Windsor on St George's Day, Edward headed north to confront yet more Lancastrian rebels in Yorkshire. On 30 April he reached Stony Stratford. The following morning he rode over to Grafton for his wedding. The romantic ceremony was performed on May Day 1464, probably at the hermitage, whose ruins stand just outside the village, west of the main road. In the words of Robert Fabyan in his Chronicle, written some 40 years after the event: 'In such pastime, in very secret manner, upon the first day of May, King Edward espoused Elizabeth, late wife of Sir John Gray, Knight, which spousailles were solemnised early in the morning, at the town of Grafton, near unto Stony Stratford; at which marriage was no person present but the spouse, the spousesse, the Duchess of Bedford, the priest and two gentlewomen and a young man to help the priest sing. After which spousailles ended he went to bed and so tarried there upon three or four hours, and after departed and rode again to Stony Stratford, and came in manner as though he had been hunting. And within a day or two after he sent to Grafton, to the Lord Rivers, father unto his wife, showing to him that he would come and lodge with him a certain season, where he was received with all honour, and so tarried there by the space of four days. In which season she nightly to his bed was brought, in so secret manner that almost none but her mother was council'. With even Elizabeth's father remaining in ignorance, it is no wonder that the marriage remained a closely guarded secret.

Edward visited his new bride a number of times during the summer. He spent much of July and August at his palace at Woodstock in Oxfordshire, from where he could easily have ridden over to Grafton. On 15 July he was at Stony Stratford. News of the love match finally broke in September, when the magnates assembled at the Great Council at Reading and urged the King to consider making a suitable marriage, hoping that he would accept Warwick's candidate Bona of Savoy. To their consternation Edward calmly announced that he was already married to Dame Elizabeth Grey. The idea that a King could have married for love was unheard of in the 15th century. Polydore Vergil summed up contemporary opinion, commenting that Edward was ruled 'by blind affection and not by the rule of reason'. Despite much grumbling that her pedigree was not sufficiently grand, there was little that the nobles could do without provoking outright rebellion, although news soon spread abroad that the match was unpopular. Fabyan later commented darkly that Elizabeth's mother Jacquetta had cast a spell over the King.

On Michaelmas Day Queen Elizabeth was presented to the peers of the realm in a magnificent ceremony at Reading. More remarkable still, not only had Edward acted in defiance of his greatest counsellors and nobles, but he created Elizabeth Queen Consort. She was crowned in great splendour in Westminster Abbey on 26 May 1465. Following the announcement of the marriage, Edward showered honours on the Woodville family. Elizabeth's father was created Earl Rivers and made Lord Treasurer and Constable of England. Her sisters were married off to the leading members of the peerage. Even more scandalously, Elizabeth's youngest brother John, aged 20, wed the wealthy thrice-married Dowager Duchess of Norfolk, at least forty years his senior. Edward's court jester, with some justice, joked that 'the Rivers run so high that it is impossible to get through them'. Nevertheless, these honours were by no means exceptional, especially compared with those recently acquired by Warwick's family the Nevilles. But the earl felt that his position as the King's chief supporter was being undermined by these promotions, particularly when Edward ignored his advice and formed an alliance with Burgundy against France.

In 1469 Warwick raised the flag of revolt. On 26 July he routed the King's forces at Edgecote in Warwickshire. Hastening from the field of battle, the earl arrested Rivers and his son John, whom he particularly hated for his presumption in marrying the aged Duchess of Norfolk, probably at their home at Grafton. Father and son were taken to Northampton, where they were summarily executed without trial. The Duchess of Bedford was now charged with witchcraft and sorcery by a neighbour, Thomas Wake of Blisworth, a testament to the fear in which she was held. After a prolonged struggle, in which both Edward and Warwick, in turn, were forced to flee for their lives abroad, the King with his new Captain-General Anthony Woodville, now 2nd Earl Rivers, in the words of Baker 'one of the most valiant and accomplished noblemen of the 15th century', finally defeated his overmighty subject at the battle of Barnet on Easter Sunday 1471. The Kingmaker fell on the field of battle.

While Edward IV lived, the Woodvilles continued to bask in royal favour. In 1473 the cultured Rivers, an early patron of William Caxton, was appointed governor to the young Edward, Prince of Wales. A decade later, on Edward IV's death on 9 April 1483, Rivers was given the task of escorting the new King from Ludlow to London, where he was to be crowned on 4 May. Unfortunately, the royal party delayed their departure fatally until after the feast of St George's Day on 23 April. When Rivers finally reached Northampton on 29 April, he sent his nephew Richard Grey, Elizabeth Woodville's son by her first marriage and half-brother of Edward V, on with his royal charge to Stony Stratford for the night, passing through Grafton *en route*. During the evening Rivers dined amicably with the Duke of Gloucester, the future Richard III, who had raced down from his power base in the north to intercept the royal party, and the Duke of Buckingham. Once Rivers had retired, however, the gates of the inn in Northampton were locked. When the earl, suspecting treachery, protested, Gloucester and Buckingham had no hesitation in placing him under arrest.

The two dukes, together with their retainers and Edward's close friend Lord Hastings, who had quarrelled with the Woodvilles, mounted their horses and galloped down the road to Stony Stratford, passing through Grafton in the early hours. Reaching Stony Stratford in the morning, they were just in time to seize Edward as he was about to set forth for London. His companions were arrested. The royal party returned through Grafton to Northampton, where Gloucester replaced the young King's attendants with his own, 'at which dealing he (Edward) wept and was nothing content, but it booted not'. The date was 30 April, nineteen years to the day since Edward's father, smitten with love, had arrived at Stony Stratford on the eve of his wedding. Richard had no such romantic illusions, and ordered Rivers to be taken to Pontefract, where he was beheaded.

Grafton was to feature once more in the Wars of the Roses. Gloucester's *coup d'état* was successful, once he had persuaded Queen Elizabeth to deliver up her younger son Richard to join his brother Edward in the Tower of London, and he swiftly declared himself King Richard III. But, following the announcement of the death of the Princes in the Tower, revolts broke out all over England. Richard moved to the Midlands to meet the threat and on 19 October halted at Grafton Manor. Although the 'bottled spider', as he was nicknamed, was successful in crushing the revolt, his ruthless behaviour continued to attract adherents to Henry Tudor, the heir of the House of Lancaster, who was living in exile in Brittany. Among these was Richard Woodville, 3rd Earl Rivers, Elizabeth Woodville's last surviving brother. In the late summer of 1485 Henry landed at Milford Haven, accompanied by Rivers. The Dowager Queen, who had suffered a succession of tragic misfortunes in losing a husband, two brothers and three sons killed or murdered in the Wars of the Roses, was avenged when Richard III was killed at the battle of Bosworth on 22 August.

Elizabeth's fortunes appeared to have turned full circle when her eldest daughter Elizabeth of York married Henry VII on 18 January 1486. All subsequent monarchs are descended from this union of the houses of York and Lancaster. Rivers, meanwhile, died childless at Grafton in 1491, whereupon his title became extinct. In his will he asked his nephew and heir Thomas, Marquess of Dorset, Elizabeth's eldest son, to sell sufficient underwood from the woods at Grafton to buy a bell for the church as a memorial to the Woodvilles. A year later, on 8 June 1492, Elizabeth herself died, and was laid to rest in the recently consecrated St George's Chapel in Windsor Castle, one of the glories of English Gothic architecture, next to her husband Edward. The best likeness of her is to be found in Queens' College, Cambridge, which she had jointly founded, together with her predecessor Margaret of Anjou.

HENRY VIII

The monarch who loved Grafton most was Henry VIII, the grandson of
Edward and Elizabeth. He acquired the manor, together with that of
Hartwell, in 1527 from Thomas, 2nd Marquess of Dorset, in exchange
for the manors of Loughborough and Shepshed (Leics.). Henry VIII
loved Grafton for its sport, the falconry and fishing, but above all for the
deer hunting in the surrounding royal forest, which encompassed the
combined parks at Grafton and Potterspury, about a mile to the west of
the village, together with a new park to the north at Hartwell. He built
a magnificent house which would serve both as a hunting lodge and a
place where he could hold meetings of the Privy Council. As a measure
of Grafton's new status, the King added the epithet Regis to the village's
name.

In 1541 Grafton and Hartwell became the nucleus around which
Henry VIII created the honor of Grafton (an ancient title revived by the
King) which included a substantial portion of south Northamptonshire
and north Buckinghamshire. From 1 May 1542 the manor of Grafton was
to be the 'chief park and place' of the honor. During Henry's lifetime the
honor retained its privileged position in this area of the Midlands. Since
1541 the descent of the manor has followed the same course as that of
the honor, remaining part of the crown estate until 1706 and since then
the property of the FitzRoys, Dukes of Grafton.

The King spent several weeks at Grafton in most years of his reign,
typically arriving towards the end of August and leaving in early
October, often as part of a progress that included a visit to Ampthill
either before or afterwards. Often these visits included affairs of state.
Privy Council meetings were held at Grafton in 1540 and 1541 and
possibly in other years. The ambassadors of Hungary were received there
in 1531 and the Scottish ambassador in 1537. Sometimes the King was
prevented from visiting by the plague; there were outbreaks at Grafton
in 1528, and in 1537 he was advised against including the house on his
itinerary since the plague had reached Towcester and Buckingham, both
less than ten miles away.

Most famously, the last meeting of Henry, his chief minister and
Chancellor Thomas Wolsey and Cardinal Campeggio took place at
Grafton Manor on 19 and 20 September 1529. This occasion gives a
vivid insight into the passion and fury which lay behind Henry's decisive

15 Cardinal Thomas Wolsey (English School). Henry VIII's chief minister, whose last momentous meeting with the King was held at Grafton Manor in 1529.

break with Rome and the dangerous uncertainty surrounding this momentous event. The King had become infatuated with Anne Boleyn and was determined to divorce his wife Catherine of Aragon, who had failed to provide him with the male heir he longed for. In order to obtain the divorce Henry needed the permission of Pope Clement VII, who was in the control of Catherine's uncle, the Emperor Charles V. Cardinal Wolsey had been instructed by the King to deal with the matter. In a last desperate attempt to persuade the Pope, Wolsey invited the papal envoy, Cardinal Campeggio, to come to England to discuss matters. When the negotiations proved inconclusive, Wolsey determined on a last interview with the King at Grafton.

The final encounter took place at the Manor on the feast of the Virgin and has been vividly recorded by Wolsey's attendant and biographer George Cavendish. The Cardinal's enemies had gathered to watch his disgrace. Even before the meeting took place, they were betting on whether Henry would deign to talk to his Chancellor. When Wolsey arrived on 19 September he found that no room had been prepared for him at the royal hunting lodge. The most powerful man in England was left waiting in the courtyard like a common servant until Sir Henry Norris, the King's Groom of the Stole and chief gentleman of the Privy Chamber, offered the Cardinal his own room to change out of his travelling clothes. Norris alerted Henry to Wolsey's arrival, whereupon a number of courtiers, hedging their bets, appeared to welcome him and to discuss 'all things touching the King's displeasure towards him'. He was summoned to attend the King and Campeggio in the presence chamber. The Duke of Norfolk, the Earl of Suffolk and Anne Boleyn's father Lord Rochford, who all hated Wolsey for his arrogance and greed, gathered expectantly to watch his humiliation. The Cardinal entered the chamber in trepidation and knelt before the King. But, to his opponents' chagrin, Henry greeted his former favourite 'with as amiable a cheer as ever', and led him to the window embrasure, where they were soon deep in conversation. However, their talk was not completely amicable and the King was overheard saying: 'How can that be? Is this not your own hand?'. Henry then withdrew to dine privately with his mistress.

Anne Boleyn, who harboured a virulent hatred of Wolsey, was enraged by this turn of events. She had set her heart on becoming Queen of England and, in Cavendish's words, already 'kept state more like a Queen than a simple maid'. At dinner she appeared 'much offended', and launched into an attack on the errant Cardinal: 'Sir, is it not a marvellous thing to consider what debts and danger the Cardinal hath brought you in with all your subjects?' 'How so sweetheart?', asked the King innocently, to which Anne replied hotly: 'Forsooth there is not a man

ANNA . BOLEYN · REGINA ANGLIÆ . 1534

16 Anne Boleyn (English School). Henry VIII's second wife and mother of Elizabeth I. Deeply hostile to Wolsey, and present at his final interview with the King at Grafton Manor.

within your realm worth five pounds, but the Cardinal indebted you unto him by his means', a reference to Wolsey's most unpopular tax. To press the point home, she continued: 'There is never a nobleman within this realm that if he had done half so much as the Cardinal hath done, he were well worthy to lose his head. If my lord Norfolk, my lord Suffolk, my lord my father or any other noble person within your realm had done much less than he, they should have lost their heads by now'. Henry, continuing to play the innocent, responded: 'Why then, I perceive that you are not the Cardinal's friend', to which his mistress replied wrathfully: 'Forsooth, Sir, I have no cause, nor any other that loves your Grace, if ye consider well his doings'.

After dinner the King appeared to ignore his mistress's argument and once again was to be seen deep in conversation with Wolsey 'very secretly'. But Anne used all her wiles to turn her lover against his minister once the couple had retired for the night. As there was no bedroom for the Chancellor, he was compelled to stay at the nearby mansion of Easton Neston. Next morning, Wolsey returned to Grafton but was not invited to join the royal hunting party. Although 'the King departed amiably in the sight of all men', Anne Boleyn ensured that the hunt lasted all day, and the Cardinal left for London without having another chance to speak with Henry. He was never to see his royal master again. Within a month, he had been stripped of all his titles and endured the ignominy of his rivals Norfolk and Suffolk coming in person to his lodgings to seize the seals of office. Meanwhile Campeggio had left for the Continent, having failed to bring about an agreement, and the break with Rome followed shortly afterwards. Anne did not live long to enjoy her success. When she failed to produce a male heir, she fell into disgrace. It was she, not Wolsey, who was to die on the scaffold.

Henry continued to favour Grafton. He brought his fifth wife Katherine Howard here in 1540. The King, now an ailing and obese figure, had fallen headlong for the delectable 15-year-old, charmingly attired in the most fashionable French clothes. For the first few months of marriage he was barely able to let her out of his sight. They arrived at Grafton on 29 August. The French ambassador, Charles de Marillac, who was a spectator, recorded Henry's infatuation: 'The King is so amorous of her that he cannot treat her well enough, and caresses her more than he did the others. The new Queen is a lady of moderate beauty but superlative grace. In stature she is small and slender. Her countenance is very delightful, of which the King is so greatly enamoured, and he knows not how to make sufficient demonstrations of his affections for her'. They enjoyed a blissful stay until 7 September and the King signalled his happiness by ordering a gold medal to be struck with Tudor roses and lovers' knots entwined. However, like her predecessor Anne Boleyn, Katherine Howard was executed when the King discovered that she had been unfaithful to him.

The Manor

Grafton Manor, in which these stirring events took place, was presumably built by the Woodville family during the period in which they were tenants of either the Poles or, before 1348, Grestain abbey. Although there appear to be no medieval references to the house, it is clear from the earliest accounts of work done at Grafton immediately after Henry VIII acquired the estate that an existing house was being repaired, not a new one being built from scratch. In 1528–9 stone and other materials were removed from the old castle at Castlethorpe (Bucks.) and timber taken from the royal parks at Hanslope and elsewhere to refurbish Grafton. Further work was done in 1536–7, when new chimneys were added to the house and a bowling alley built close to the churchyard, enclosed by a wall 14 ft high, with the alley itself defined by banks made from potters' clay dug at Potterspury. A great wrought-iron folding gate was installed next to the church on the street side. In 1539 it was noted that there was roofing timber, lead and slate at three recently suppressed religious houses in Northampton that might be suitable for Grafton, but there is no evidence of further work at the house until 1541, when a campaign began that continued until 1543, coinciding with the creation of the honor of Grafton. There was renewed expenditure at Grafton in 1545–8, although much of this was probably spent on lodges, palings and other works in the adjoining parks.

A gallery was constructed for Henry VIII. Its alignment was determined by the topography, the northern side following the break of slope where the land falls away northward into West Church Field, already an area of pasture in the mid 16th century. The gallery extended from very close to the eastern boundary of Grafton Park, although there is no suggestion that the former ever gave access to the latter. The construction of the gallery may have required the closure of a back road to the north side of the village and its diversion to run along the southern side of the gallery to join the main street. In the 1650 survey the gallery is shown to have extended, like the earthwork today, almost to the main road. It may possibly have served as a cover for Henry to walk to his hunting lodge.

The Park

Once Grafton passed to the Crown in 1527 Henry VIII decided to create a large hunting park of almost a thousand acres by massively expanding the medieval park, combining it with the nearby Potterspury and Plum parks, of which only a third was in the parish of Grafton. The park extended right up to the Northampton road and adjoined the gardens of Grafton Manor.

The new park formed a large rectangle and had slight ramparts on the north, only well-preserved near Plum Park, 3 m. wide without a ditch at SP 7350 4574. At the south-east, the boundary is formed by a large rampart. The enlargement of Grafton Park was part of a large-scale planning process in the region. Paulerspury, Stoke Bruerne and Hartwell Parks were also enlarged, and the last formed a connection to Salcey Forest. To join Grafton Park to Hartwell, the land to the north of Grafton village was enclosed as pasture, thus providing an unbroken tract of forest, parks and enclosures from Kings Hill near Syresham to Pidding-ton woods (13 miles), available for hunting without any interruption by arable crops.

This major piece of emparking is documented in part through Henry's privy purse expenses for 1531–2 which record payments to the keepers of Grafton and Potterspury as well as other nearby parks. In the latter year he ordered that Grafton Park be extended northward by the addition of 70 acres from the fields of Alderton and 76 acres from those of Grafton where the park extended right up to the edge of the village, including the site of the chantry. Five years later 150 acres were added to Potterspury Park, so that it now joined Grafton Park on its northern edge. In 1543 payments were made to freeholders whose lands had been enclosed in both parks, and for the cost of making a new pond in Potterspury Park. By 1558 it was estimated that the parks held 500 deer each.

The King took a close interest in the sport at Grafton, issuing orders for hunting to the keepers of the nearby forests, and to his falconer, referring to 'a brace of greyhounds out of Wales', and instructing the butts for archery to be prepared. He also went fishing at Grafton. His accounts record a payment of 15s. to Michael Pylleson 'that gave an angle-rodde unto the King's grace at Grafton'. Henry enjoyed the local produce, was happy to pay for cucumbers brought from his garden at Beaulieu, and to give money 'to a poor woman that gave the king's grace pears and nuts in the forest'.

Grafton Lodge

This major new building shows the importance Henry attached to his visits to Grafton. It stands on newly emparked land about a quarter of a mile west of the village. This is the only survivor of the two lodges

Henry is recorded as constructing in the new park. The building was probably erected in the 1530s or early 1540s since there are records of repairs carried out to the lodge and to the two parks of Grafton and Potterspury in 1546.

The surviving lodge is built of a mixture of coursed, squared limestone, ironstone and brick. The house was originally **T**-shaped in plan, with the main entrance facing east towards the Manor. The brickwork has an interesting diaper pattern on the south front and three rectangular patterns in blue brick on the north front. A chamfered plinth runs round the exterior at the height of three feet. Three massive 16th-century brick chimney stacks rise above the roof. Despite alterations and additions in the 19th and 20th centuries, the interior preserves a fine inglenook fireplace with a Tudor privy adjoining. The scale and quality of the lodge indicate that this was almost certainly built for members of the royal party accompanying the King on his visits to Grafton.

ELIZABETH I

The Manor

No later sovereign showed as much interest in Grafton as Henry VIII, but his daughter Elizabeth I visited the village on three occasions, in 1564, 1568 and in June and July 1575. The Queen liked to make a progress every summer outside London during the first two decades of her reign. In 1568 the Spanish ambassador reported how 'She was received everywhere with great acclamations and signs of joy as is customary in this country whereat she was exceedingly pleased'. Elizabeth was accompanied by a vast household comprising a Lord Steward, a controller and an army of clerks, cooks, bakers, ushers, grooms, maids and pages, and a baggage train of 200–300 carts.

These progresses were not solely for pleasure. The Queen was attended by her Council, numbering between 17 and 20 of the chief officers of state. In 1575 she held a series of Council meetings in Grafton Manor, described as the queen's 'stately honor house' in 1558, the year of her succession. The tenant of the Manor was then Elizabeth's glamorous favourite Robert Dudley, Earl of Leicester. In 1574 he paid 100 marks for a lease of the demesnes at £42 12s. 11d. p.a. Leicester was adept at flattering the Queen, and told her that of the places she would be staying at on her progress, none would be 'more pleasant and healthful' than Grafton, which she had ordered to be repaired and which would be made ready for her. Leicester authorised his protégé William Spicer to supervise work costing the vast sum of £1,842 between 1573 and 1575 in preparation for the Queen's stay during the summer of that year. Old buildings were repaired but the principal work was a 'new building', containing two floors and covered by four roofs. This contrasts with a number of lesser repairs, costing some £170 in 1551–3, £450 in 1553–4, and a further £396 in 1585–6.

Leicester described Elizabeth's visit in 1575 in a letter to Sir William Cecil, later Lord Burghley, the Queen's chief minister, who had preceded him as tenant of the Manor. It was a beautiful summer's day when the Queen arrived at Grafton Regis, 'being a marvellous hot day at her coming', he wrote, and 'there was not a drop of good drink for her'. The Queen was much put out by the lack of water after her journey, and even Leicester blanched at the ale on offer: 'No man was able to drink it; you

17 Elizabeth I by Marcus Gheeraerts the Younger (the Ditchley Portrait). Elizabeth was the guest of her paramour the Earl of Leicester on a celebrated visit to Grafton in 1575.

had been as good to have drunk Malmsey. It did put me out of temper'. Fortunately, some light ale was found and he ended on a more cheerful note: 'God be thanked, she is now perfect well and merry'. The visit to Grafton served as a foretaste for the extravagant reception Leicester had arranged for his beloved Elizabeth at his castle at Kenilworth in Warwickshire. The scene of enchantment must have dazzled the 11-year-old William Shakespeare, who came to watch it from nearby Stratford and provided much of the inspiration when he came to write *A Midsummer Night's Dream* some twenty years later.

The Honor of Grafton

Leicester and Cecil were two of a number of important nobles who leased the demesne of the manor, the most valuable part of the honor of Grafton, during the later 16th century and early 17th. They succeeded John Williams, created Lord Williams of Thame in 1554, who paid £60 a year for numerous offices, including steward, bailiff and keeper of Grafton Manor, master forester and master of the deer hunt in Whittlewood forest. By 1558 the land of the manor of Grafton, which had been kept in hand by Henry VIII, was being leased in parcels. As elsewhere within the honor, tenants were induced to surrender and pay a fine for renewal well before the expiry of their leases, which were normally for 21 years. This appears to have led to the consolidation and enclosure of a large area of demesne (the land attached to the manor house) to the north of the village, amounting to about 600 acres in the 17th century, which became known as Grafton Pastures.

Two other farms were leased to John Kirby, one for his own occupation and the other for his son, and three others, together with seven cottages and some land, were leased to William Parr, Marquess of Northampton. A notable feature of these leases is the regularity of farm size: all five holdings had 36 acres of common field land (i.e. one virgate), 2½ acres of leys and 2 or 2½ acres of meadow. There were no copyholders (i.e. those holding by a grant made by the manor court) by the mid 16th century. George Ferne replaced Northampton as tenant of his holdings in 1574, on payment of a fine of two years' rent. A decade later the three farms leased to Ferne were granted out separately to the occupiers in return for fines of one or two years' rent. In 1575 John Kirby's assignee, Lawrence Manley, was granted a new 21-year lease in return for a similar fine; Manley's lease was surrendered after only five years to enable the premises to be divided between him and Henry Lumbard. In 1581 Leicester paid £20 for a renewal of his lease.

JAMES I AND CHARLES I

The Manor

When James VI of Scotland succeeded to the English throne in 1603, he distributed many of the most lucrative positions in his patronage to the Scottish nobles who accompanied him south to his new kingdom. These included his cousin Ludovic Stuart, 2nd Duke of Lennox, son of James's first great favourite and probable lover Esme Stuart. Lennox was made steward of the honor of Grafton in 1605 despite a claim the Earl of Cumberland possessed on the title. In a letter written in late October 1605 to his chief minister Robert Cecil, Earl of Salisbury, whose father Lord Burghley had been tenant of the Manor, James praised Cecil's discretion in giving Lennox the position which was obviously much sought after. 'My little beagle', he began, 'Ye cannot think how great a pleasure ye did me in your discreet dealing with Cumberland, whereby ye relieved me out of a strait that could not but have fashit (bothered) me'. Within days, the King owed his life to 'his little beagle' after Cecil discovered Guy Fawkes and the Gunpowder Plot on the eve of the opening of Parliament.

James I stayed at the Manor at Grafton in 1608, 1610, 1612, 1614 and again in August 1616, indulging his consuming passion for hunting deer, which was noted by the Venetian ambassador: 'He seems to have forgotten he is King except in his kingly pursuit of Stags to which he is foolishly devoted'. James, however, emulated his predecessors in mixing business with pleasure. In August 1612 he was corresponding from Grafton with Sir Thomas Edmondes in France, recording the growing influence of the pro-Spanish and anti-Protestant party following the assassination of Henri IV two years earlier. By this date the Duke of Lennox seems to have come to some arrangement with the Earl of Cumberland regarding the use of the Manor.

Despite the royal visits, Grafton Manor gradually fell into decay and some dismantling took place. At the same time minor repairs were carried out and the house must have remained habitable. The month before the King's visit in 1616 a Scottish courtier named Sir George Keire obtained a sign manual for a grant of the materials of the house and a lease of the site, although this appears not to have taken effect, since shortly afterwards the honor was included in the estates granted to

18 James I by Cornelius Jonson. The King came to Grafton Regis several times to enjoy the hunting.

the newly created Prince of Wales. The honor had previously been granted to Prince Henry, James I's eldest son, who died in 1612. The grant to Prince Charles, however, implies that the house was in decay and this was confirmed in 1619 when the Prince's chancellor gave instructions to his surveyor to board up the new buildings at Grafton, where they were exposed to the elements, using in part old materials.

A few years after Charles became King in 1625 the honor of Grafton, including the mansion, was mortgaged to Sir Francis Crane, who was in the process of commissioning Inigo Jones, the leading architect in the newly imported Italian Renaissance style, to build a splendid house nearby at Stoke Park, another house on the Crown estate. Crane is chiefly remembered for setting up the Mortlake tapestry works in 1619, an attempt to rival the great tapestry works at Brussels. At Grafton, Crane decided to use the outbuildings of the manor, whose stone was valued at the enormous price of £4,000, as a quarry for his own mansion at Stoke Park, soon to become one of the architectural jewels of Northamptonshire. Sir Robert Osborne, who leased the adjoining land, lamented the destruction of Grafton Manor, 'the best and bravest seat in the kingdom, a seat fit for a prince and not a subject'.

Whatever the truth of the allegations, the Manor evidently remained habitable. In the early 1630s the Earls of Cumberland, continuing their association with Grafton, rented the house as a staging-post on their journeys between London and the North. Large parties must have stayed there, judging from the household accounts of the Cliffords, where 'not only pasties of red deer venison were sent thither by express from Skipton; but carcases of staggs, two, four, or more, at once, were baked whole, and dispatched to the same place'. By this date the village was moving towards the main road, with four cottages being built on the waste ground adjoining the road. In 1630 there is a record of five alehouses in Grafton, indicating the village's increasing prosperity.

In 1638 Dame Mary Crane, Sir Francis's widow, after prolonged litigation, secured a grant of the Manor for her life in return for the surrender of an earlier lease. Two years later she is recorded as sending a gift of poultry to the courtier Endymion Porter and his wife. She was still at Grafton in December 1643, when the manor was garrisoned for the King by Sir John Digby.

Grafton Park

Despite the neglect of the buildings of Grafton, the land around the village continued to be enclosed. In 1605 Plum Park was enclosed and united with the two larger parks of Grafton and Potterspury to the west, when the total perimeter of the three was said to be eight miles; three years later a payment of £333 9s. 6d. was authorised to Thomas Hasilrigg, then lessee of Alderton demesnes, for woodlands to be added to Grafton and Potterspury parks; and in 1611 Sir Arthur Throckmorton and other tenants in Paulerspury were paid £50 for ground conveyed to the king for enlarging Grafton Park.

The effect of these changes was to create a single estate which extended from Watling Street in the south-west to the Northampton road at Grafton, bounded on the north-west by the common fields of Alderton and Paulerspury, and on the south-east by those of Grafton and Yardley. These boundaries, probably established by 1620 if not a little earlier, remained unchanged until well into the 19th century. The estate as a whole was known as Grafton Park, although the distinction between Grafton Park and Potterspury (or Pury) Park survived well after the land itself had been disparked. There were two principal houses on the estate, Grafton Lodge and Potterspury Lodge, and at least two of the families that owned the estate in the 17th and early 18th centuries lived at the latter, rather than the house from which the estate took its name.

Both lodges are shown on a map of the Grafton Park estate of 1721. At Potterspury, the lodge lies within the inferred boundary of the medieval park but the present Grafton Lodge stands on the 16th-century extension to the park. Repairs to the lodge at Grafton and to both parks were specified among work done at the honor of Grafton in 1619, and in 1637 Charles I was advised that the 'Great Lodge' in Grafton Park was so badly decayed that it would be better to take it down than repair it. The paling of both parks was in urgent need of attention to safeguard the deer, for which 100 oaks and £60 would be needed. Sir Charles Harbord, the Surveyor-General of Woods and Forests, was to be given the money and was himself to give orders to fell the trees needed for the work. The following year, another 70 oaks were still needed to complete the repairs at Grafton, which were to be obtained from either Whittle-wood or Salcey forests. Coppices in Grafton Park were regularly felled and sold in this period.

Grafton and Potterspury Parks remained part of the honor of Grafton until the reign of Charles I and a succession of courtiers received grants of the keepership of the two parks, with a fee of 2d. a day, plus herbage (right of pasture on another's land), pannage (right of pasturage of pigs) and fallen wood. From 1622 to 1628 the office was held by George Villiers, Duke of Buckingham, the powerful favourite of James I and Charles I. He was succeeded by Sir William Washington and his wife Anne, while the Earl of Dorset held the office of high steward of the honor of Grafton. By 1633 a fresh grant was made to Sir Francis Crane and Anne Washington, with reversion to Dorset. Crane was at this date involved in negotiations to lend £7,500 on security of a mortgage of the honor.

As Charles I's financial problems worsened in the 1640s, the Grafton Park estate was seen as a convenient means of raising further sums. In 1641 the King made a grant to Thomas Marsham and Ferdinand of London of the office of keeper of Grafton and Potterspury parks for life, with the usual stipend of 2d. a day and rights of herbage and pannage, and the browse wood (young shoots as fodder for cattle), windfalls and dead wood, with the reversion of the offices to the Earl of Dorset.

THE CIVIL WAR SIEGE
OF GRAFTON REGIS

By Glenn Foard

At the outbreak of hostilities in August 1642 Northampton was fortified as a major parliamentarian garrison. However, following the battle of Edgehill in October, Banbury fell to the royalists and until May 1646 they held the castle there as an outpost of the King's capital at Oxford. The south-western part of Northamptonshire was therefore a disputed territory and throughout the war the people were at times taxed by both the county committee at Northampton and the royalist garrison at Banbury. Buckinghamshire was controlled from the parliamentarian garrison at Aylesbury, but the north-west of the county was another disputed territory. Though the greater part of these areas were normally under parliamentarian control, the territory around Grafton Regis suffered various raids by the Banbury garrison and other royalist forces.

1643 was the King's most successful year of the war and that autumn his main field army returned to Oxford to take up winter quarters. With such large numbers of troops at hand Prince Rupert, the King's senior commander, had the opportunity for a major local campaign to capture the south Midlands. Parliament had commanded most of this wealthy and populous region since the beginning of the war, giving them control of the strategically important roads running from London to the Midlands and the North. On 14 October 1643 Rupert advanced with 2,000 horse and 700 foot, hoping to take Northampton by treachery, but the garrison had been forewarned and the royalists were driven off. Rather than retreat, Rupert marched on into the Ouse valley to plunder north Bedfordshire and Buckinghamshire, before fortifying the small market town of Newport Pagnell to consolidate his control of the area. This was a challenge to which Parliament simply had to respond. The London trained bands were mobilised under the veteran commander Major-General Sir Philip Skippon to drive out the royalists. On receiving the news of Skippon's advance on 27 October, the royalist commander of Newport Pagnell slighted the newly constructed defences and fell back towards Banbury. Skippon took control of Newport and re-fortified the town, establishing a garrison which was to remain in parliamentarian hands throughout the rest of the war.

Rupert took control of the next significant town, Towcester, which would enable him to retain at least part of the territory that had been gained and, since it stood astride Watling Street, then the most important road in England, it gave him control of communications from London to the Midlands. Local people were drafted in from many miles around to fortify the town. There were some 14 regiments quartered in Towcester and the surrounding villages and by late November it was reported that the royalists 'hath made it very strong, and brought the water round about the towne …'. The impact of such a major army on the surrounding countryside was dramatic. A parliamentarian news-sheet reported that 'The enemie at Tositer drive the fields of all Cattell, and thresh out the peoples corne of all sorts, forcing the Countrey-men to doe it; poore Northamptonshire, especially the West division, as thou hast been a faithfull peece to the parliament, so have thy miseries been great, what they reward hereafter may be, God knowes: alas, what pitty does the Kings party shew thee, or any destroyed part of poore England'. Another report claimed that 'the popish army there having manifested their basenesse so much, as that children can scarce get a piece of bread but it is taken from them, and the Children left to perish'.

A Garrison at Grafton Regis

The Northampton garrison of 1,500 men was no match for the main royalist field army, but together with the London trained bands they were able to make surprise attacks on the enemy quarters in the villages around Towcester, as on 2 November, when there were skirmishes at Alderton and Stowe Nine Churches. However, if the royalists were to be driven out, then a major offensive was required. Instead, during November Rupert further strengthened his grip on the region by establishing lesser garrisons at Hillesden House near Buckingham and Boarstall House near Brill. Then, on 14 November, came the first report that Colonel Sir John Digby was at Grafton Regis with a regiment of horse and a further 400 horse at Paulerspury. The Digbys were described in parliamentarian propaganda as a papist family, one of Sir John's brothers being close to the King while his father had been executed for his involvement in the Gunpowder Plot. He was joined by 'Sir John Waycutt' (probably Sir John Wake of Hartwell), and by 19 November they had begun to fortify Lady Crane's house at Grafton. The Cranes were also royalist supporters, Lady Crane's chaplain, Thomas Bunning, having already been ejected from his living at Grafton by the Northampton Committee because of his papist leanings. By fortifying the manor house at Grafton the royalists now also controlled the main road from London to Northampton and Leicester.

Digby forced men from the surrounding villages 'to come and helpe to digg and make bulwarks'. By late December the garrison was described, probably with some exaggeration, as 'a place of great strength and consequence', with fortifications encompassing both Grafton House and the church. The garrison was strengthened with infantry by 1 December while the cavalry were quartered half a mile distant from the house, perhaps at the lodge in the park. By mid December there were 100 musketeers, 300 cavalry and three artillery pieces in the garrison with two more expected. By the time of the siege there were six pieces of artillery within the defences, perhaps placed on the bulwarks which had been constructed in the preceding weeks. The accounts of the men and arms taken when Digby surrendered show the garrison had been reorganised some time in mid December, leaving 14 officers, five being of the horse and nine of the foot, together with 100 musketeers and 80 cavalry troopers. In addition to fortifying the house the garrison also posted a sentry at Castlethorpe bridge, which was the nearest crossing of the river Tove leading to the parliamentarian garrison at Newport Pagnell, while '2 troopes of horse come forth every night to see if the contry bee cleere and returne to their quarters'.

Any garrison needed an effective mechanism for supply and hence by late November Grafton began drawing taxes from the surrounding countryside, in both Northamptonshire and Buckinghamshire. On 26 November 'Sir John Digby was at Hanslopp (3 miles from Nuport) with a party of horse. There hee layd a taxe upon the towne that they should provid £5 a day to bee brought in to them every third day. Tuesday being the day of payment they being fearful to stay in the town came to Newport ... '. It was reported on 1 December that the royalists at Grafton 'sendeth out dayly into the country to bring in fether bedds to them'. At this time Digby was drawing some £250 per week from the Northamptonshire hundred of Cleley alone.

In early December Rupert marched back to Oxford with most of the army, to provide support for Hopton's campaign in the south, but contrary to some reports there was no intention to abandon the territory so recently gained. The defences of both Towcester and Grafton had been completed and a garrison left in each. However, there were problems for the garrisons, the commander of Towcester complaining on 16 December that only three hundreds (Towcester, Norton and Cleley) had been allocated for the support of the Towcester garrison, the rest having been withdrawn for the use of the Banbury garrison since the departure of the bulk of the army from Towcester. Moreover, the long residence of so many horse in the two hundreds around the town meant many of the people were unable to pay much, while Cleley Hundred was controlled by Sir John Digby for the support of the Grafton garrison. His assessment was that 'unless there be means found to supply this garrison with a weekly supply of three hundred pounds, it will be altogether impossible to preserve it'. Most important, for the first time since October the royalists in the area were severely outnumbered.

Grafton Regis in 1643

Unlike most neighbouring parishes, the greater part of Grafton Regis had been enclosed in large hedged fields and converted to pasture in the 16th century. The medieval deer park was also enormously expanded first by Henry VIII and later by James I, extending right up to the Northampton road, to the very edge of the village. The park was in part enclosed by a pale (a timber palisade) as well as a hedge and ditch but in other places just by a pale. The new divisions of the park were almost wholly pasture, that next to the village having only 569 trees, with just one small coppice at the north-east corner, compared with 5,725 trees in the south-west division, which included the medieval park. Hence by 1643 much of the land surrounding Grafton was enclosed by hedgerows, providing a very different context for military action to the open landscape which was to be found across most of Northamptonshire. At Grafton the open fields were restricted to just a few hundred acres on the south side of the parish. The immediate area, though it provided good grazing for the horses, was not particularly well-suited to cavalry action but provided cover for infantry.

The village itself, lying along a quite steep spur of land protruding out into the Tove valley at the point where the main road from London to Northampton crossed the ridge, was ideally suited as a garrison. It had never been a large settlement and had shrunk since the medieval period. By the 1640s there were no more than eight 'messuages', of which only four were substantial farms, and nine cottages. Grafton had expanded westward in the 16th century on to the Northampton road, attracted by the commercial opportunities of passing traffic, so that by the mid 17th century most of the houses lined both sides of the main road. Of these, one was an inn, the King's Arms, and three others were alehouses, one of which doubled up as a smithy. Grafton was thus a significant staging-post for long-distance travellers on this major route. In addition there was the manor house itself, the church and the rectory, now somewhat isolated from most of the rest of the village.

Grafton House, which provided the core of the garrison, had been an important royal residence, though by 1643 it was much decayed from the time when Henry VIII was a frequent visitor. By the early 17th century it had begun to fall into decay and the estate was leased out to various tenants. In 1628 James I mortgaged Grafton, together with other lands in Stoke Bruerne and elsewhere, to Sir Francis Crane. Sir Francis died in 1636 but his wife Mary was granted Grafton House for life in 1638 at a yearly rent of 10s. She was certainly in residence in 1641. The only survival today of the great house is a single building against the main street just west of the churchyard, part of the former stable, kitchen and brewhouse. Recent excavations immediately to the north-east of this have revealed extensive spreads of demolition rubble from the great house but none of the foundations have yet been located to show exactly where the main buildings stood. Thus, despite the detailed Tudor descriptions, we do not know the extent or layout of the house and hence the degree to which it provided the defenders with commanding fire over the surrounding land. On the western side of the site is a substantial earthwork bank which formed the northern extent of a Tudor garden feature known as 'The Gallery' in 1650, a walled enclosure later described as the Warren, 'bounded with a large wall of Bricke and Stone ... '. The massive bank will probably prove to be simply part of this gallery rather than defensive works constructed around the house in 1643, for it lies so far from the house.

The defences are likely to have enclosed an area of no more than perhaps 100 m. by 200 m., for a circuit much larger would have been very difficult to defend with a small garrison. They probably encompassed just the churchyard and part of the manor house grounds, bounded by the road on the east and south, for the church tower and the walls of the house were to serve as the main firing position for the defending troops. Unfortunately, not only are we uncertain as to the exact location and layout of Henry VIII's great house, neither has any trace of Digby's defensive bank or ditch yet been recognised to show where the fortifications ran or the scale of the defences. However, given that no more than five weeks were available for their construction, they are unlikely to have been particularly substantial, and probably consisted of a fairly small ditch with a bank revetted with turf. The main effort may well have been in the construction of the 'bulwarks', typically pointed bastions projecting forward from the walls or ramparts to provide covering. It is possible that immediately adjacent houses were demolished to give a clear field of fire but there is no record of such demolition, which was often avoided until the last minute and, if the garrison was not expecting an imminent attack, they may not have had time to complete any demolition before the enemy arrived.

The house and church were in a commanding position, looking directly over large pasture fields on the north and arable open fields on the south, and so attack would be unlikely from these directions. To the east, however, there was the parsonage and several small hedged closes to provide cover for attacking troops, while an approach would also have been partly covered because the ground falls away relatively rapidly beyond the parsonage down to the River Tove. However, the church tower would have enabled defenders to provide covering fire over much of this land and, most important, there is only a very small area at this end of the spur from which attackers could have fired upon the garrison. By far the weakest side for the garrison would have been the western approach along the ridge. There were a few buildings in close proximity to the manor house in 1650 and, unless the defences were drawn very wide or the houses demolished and later rebuilt after the siege, then these buildings would have provided excellent cover, enabling attacking troops to approach very close towards the house. Between these buildings and the other part of the village, concentrated along the main road, there was a substantial gap providing a significant field of fire for the defenders. Similarly the gallery, which was enclosed by a large stone wall, may also have provided a defensive position for the garrison. On the other hand, the houses along the main road, the park pale which lined the west side of the road, and the hedged fields lining both sides of the road to the north, together with a small coppice at the north-east corner of the park, would have provided excellent cover for an attacking force, who would have had easy access into the park and along this ridge from the Alderton to Potterspury road.

The Siege

Preparations for the attack on Grafton were probably underway during mid December, for we find the Northampton scouts on various journeys to surrounding garrisons and towns in the days leading up to and during the siege, presumably assisting in the coordination of action. On 20 December the Northampton horse attacked royalist infantry near Grafton, but it was not until 8 p.m. on 21 December that the order went out for 1,000 infantry with four artillery pieces to march out of Newport at 2 a.m. the next day. At Lathbury, just a mile from the town, they were joined by cavalry under Colonel Norwich, a Northamptonshire commander, which provided a vanguard and rearguard. In all Skippon had under his command some 3,000 troops. They comprised the Orange and the Green regiments of the London trained bands, which he had brought up from London in the initial move against Newport Pagnell, supported by more than 1,000 troops from the Eastern Association, under the command of the Earl of Manchester, with four artillery pieces, and Colonel Norwich's regiment of horse. Some of the troops were under the command of Colonel Williams, though it is unclear which these were. They would be joined later by local troops, the main contingent coming from Northampton, said to have numbered some 1,400 horse and foot under the garrison commander, Colonel Whetham. So many were withdrawn from Northampton that it left the garrison short of men forcing the remaining troops to do double duty. Other troops, under the command of Colonel Meldrum, were draw in from the Warwick garrison.

The mobilisation of civilians in support of the siege was also quite extensive. For example, Burton Latimer, more than 20 miles away, provided one horse and man 'at the taking of Grafton House' at a cost of 6s. 8d. As one of the main supply bases in the region, Northampton was obviously involved on a large scale. Payments are recorded there for oats and cereal and for bringing the 'carigs' to Grafton House at a cost of 21s. 6d. in December 1643. Then in the period from 24 December to 15 January there are payment for bullets that had been 'bought of soldiers' and taken to Grafton House. A substantial proportion of the supplies, however, were probably provided by the villages in the area surrounding Grafton. Hence the constable of Hartwell reported later with regard to the costs to the villagers during the siege, that 'what provisons they sent thither they cannott tell'. At Stoke Bruerne the constable reported various losses: 'Richard Plowman had two horses taken from him by the Souldiers under the command of Colonel Meldrum when Grafton house was be siedged worth £10', while Robert Bond lost one mare at the same time and William Britten another, taken by Warwick soldiers, both worth £5. Without doubt, however, it was the villagers of Grafton itself who suffered the greatest losses during the siege as can be seen by the extensive claim submitted after the war by the constable of Grafton (see Appendix 1).

On the Friday morning the parliamentarian forces marched first to Grafton, which they faced, but 'leaving it on our right hand, we marcht towards Tositer, as though we had been bound thitherward'. Their march was probably via Castlethorpe bridge, approaching Grafton from the south but then turning west, perhaps through Alderton, and on to Watling Street to march north towards Towcester. About a mile from Towcester they were joined by the Northampton forces. They then faced about, so

19 Civil War engagement. The siege of Grafton Manor in December 1643 played an important part in the struggle for supremacy between the King and Parliament in the Midlands.

that the Orange Regiment were now the vanguard and Colonel William's troops the rearguard of the troops from Newport. One account claims that Skippon's first objective had been Towcester itself, saying that he had been incorrectly informed that the town was not well manned or strongly fortified, but realising the true difficulty of taking the garrison he retreated, diverting his forces against the smaller garrison at Grafton House. This seems very unlikely given the excellent intelligence which Sir Samuel Luke was gaining from his scouts during November and December. It is more likely that Grafton was his primary target because another account says that Skippon 'also sent a party to face Towciter, that so he might prevent all reliefe from comming to them'.

It is just six miles from Newport to Grafton, less than two hours journey by horse, but with the circuitous approach via Towcester it took 12 or 14 hours from the original rendezvous before they reached Grafton, arriving in the afternoon of Friday 22 December. The Eastern Association troops immediately made the first infantry assault, perhaps hoping for some element of surprise: 'when we came within sight of the house, the old souldiers of my Lord outmarcht us, and gave onset on the house very couragiously and were bravely answered, and by reason of the strength of the walls, and well fortifying of the same our Musquetiers did them small injury at that time ... '.

The first objective of the attackers would have been to take the houses and closes along the main road where some defending troops may have been deployed to stop a parliamentarian approach close to the manor house. The distribution of musket balls recovered during a recent survey suggests that it is here that some of the main action took place. It is most likely that this firefight represents an initial assault in which the defenders were driven back, with all the subsequent action concentrated in close proximity to the manor.

By Saturday 23rd, in response to the attack on Grafton, the royalist troops quartered in the area all retreated to the safety of Towcester, while those at Brackley withdrew closer to Oxford. The news was conveyed swiftly to Oxford because, as one of Luke's scouts reported from the city, 'Prince Robert marchd away on Sunday last (24th) with a great party of horse to releeve Sir John Digby at Grafffton, but comming too late hee returned to Oxford on Tuesday ... '. This must have been expected by Skippon and may in part explain why the siege was pursued with such urgency. With such a small and relatively lightly defended garrison the place might fall rapidly and avoid the need for the attackers to counter a relieving force.

Skippon may not have intended a long siege, given the awful winter weather and the threat of a relieving force marching up from Oxford. However, the troops needed shelter and some of the surrounding villages had to provide quarters for some of the troops when they were not on duty. Hence the Hartwell report says 'how many men and horses wee quartered during the siege att Grafton ... they cannott tell'. A substantial proportion of the troops remained in the open during the siege, and so they built 'hut ... in the field, for shelter from the foul winter weather'. Not surprisingly there were substantial quantities of wood, worth £26, taken both from Grafton Park and from the various tenements in the village for fires to keep the troops warm, for cooking and even for the construction of the huts themselves.

Following the initial attack, which failed to breach the defences, two artillery pieces were set up to bombard Grafton House. On the 23rd a scout from Newport reported that the parliamentarian forces 'lye against the Lady Crane's howse and the church' and that he had heard the ordnance discharged. Over the two days of the siege 'the Cannon and Musket played voilently upon the house; and there were 'diverse furious onsets made against it'. One of the soldiers reported that 'when any advantage could be gained against our Enemies, we made use of it'. Not surprisingly, given the appalling winter weather, the troops of the three

20 Civil War artillery. Both Cavaliers and Roundheads used cannon to great effect during the siege of Grafton Manor.

separate attacking forces in the field were rotated. Hence on the Saturday morning the London trained bands relieved the Eastern Association forces in their guard and on the Sunday morning the Northampton forces took their turn. At any one time it seems likely that well over a thousand men must have been deployed against Grafton House. As was so often the case in such situations the garrison used long muskets, presumably fowling pieces, to fire on the attackers at a distance beyond normal musket range. In particular there was one window in the House from which they fired, killing 'a survayor of the workes and a Captaine of a Troope of Horse slaine at one shot, and also a Gunner that belonged to the Sacre'.

The artillery fired against the house 'but they did not much annoy them neither' and so Skippon sent to Northampton for two more pieces of artillery to assist in the siege, explaining why 40s. was paid to 'John Allen canoneere for his extraordinarie service att Grafton etc.'. On the Saturday a saker was set up in a suitable location and it soon battered down the breastwork on the top of the house, 'which had done us much annoyance', and a window from where the garrison had fired on the attackers. Despite this, 'Sir John Digby who was commaunder in cheife would not yeild the house up upon noe condicions but when the Maior Generall had sent for 2 peeces of ordnance to Northampton and they were come to him, after 2 or 3 shoots they sounded a parly about 2 of the clocke in the afternoone ...'.

The most likely position for the artillery pieces ranged against the house will have been on the ridge top to the west of the house. They cannot have been far to the west because the range of a saker was between 200 and 1,000 yards and to have the maximum effect it would need to have been within 100 to 300 yards of the walls. There was no time for the digging of saps at Grafton, trenches to enable the attacking forces to approach close to the defences under cover, and so we must expect that the artillery were positioned just beyond effective musket range, perhaps between 200 to 400 yards from the defences. Given that a gunner on the saker was shot, the artillery must have been within range of a fowling piece in the house. This would all suggest that the parliamentarian forces had advanced to the east side of the houses on the main road, or perhaps had even taken cover between them, for they lay about 400 yards from and level with the house. Infantry attack would have been far more realistic from such a location, with an approach covered in part by the houses and walled and hedged closes. In contrast, an approach from the north or south would have been suicidal, across relatively open ground over which the house had such commanding fire. It is therefore not surprising to find that in the recent survey no musket balls have been recovered in the sloping ground to the north of the house. A small body of attacking troops does, however, seem to have been deployed at the eastern end of the village, for a small cluster of musket balls have been found on this side of the village, concentrated immediately behind the parsonage. They were probably there simply to control access along the road to Hartwell and so effectively close up the garrison and stop any escape or resupply.

The Northampton troops had taken the guard at about noon on the Sunday and so it was they that were facing the house when the garrison 'sounded a parley but through the eagerness of the Souldiers the Drum was shot, but not slaine out right whereupon they sent out a Trumpet and had parley granted for half an houre ... '. It was normal practice for drummers and trumpeters to be used as messengers in such situations, though in this case the dangers of such a task are plain to see. Digby had called for a parley because the women and children in the house were so distressed and the soldiers were unwilling to continue the resistance. This is undoubtedly a reflection as much of the weakness of the defences, and particularly of the way in which the stone or brick walls of a Tudor mansion were no match for the force of an artillery bombardment, as an indication of the lack of resolve of the defenders. Digby attempted to negotiate but his terms were unlikely to be accepted, for he had initially refused to surrender, thus forcing the parliamentarians to make a number of assaults on the house, with some losses. Moreover the attackers must have felt in a very strong position, with no immediate sign of any royalist relieving forces, and Skippon felt confident enough to demand unconditional surrender. Despite the rejection of his terms and the fact that his troops would be held prisoner rather than allowed to march out with their arms, Digby surrendered. He presumably believed that the house would soon fall and that if Skippon was forced to take it by storm there would be substantial losses on the royalist side and perhaps no quarter would be given to the defenders. Had Digby known that Prince Rupert was already on his way with a relieving force he might have attempted to hold out longer, but instead he yielded up the garrison at about 4 p.m. that day.

The parliamentarians suffered very light casualties. No more than ten or twenty men were killed, with a further ten or more wounded. As one of the soldiers involved in the siege reported, 'I thanke God that neither myselfe nor any of my souldiers are hurt, nor not one of our Regiment slaine notwithstanding we were in great danger and hazard'. A further nine parliamentarian soldiers were injured in an accident with their own powder, a not uncommon occurrence during the Civil War. On the royalist side we have no record of the number killed or injured, though it may have been very few. Local tradition is no substitute for contemporary accounts, particularly the story recorded in the village in the early 20th century that 'eleven people were killed in the drawing room of Grafton', to whom a monument in the church with two crosses was erected. Though one of Luke's scouts reported some 300 common soldiers as well as four or five colonels had been taken, the prisoner list shows this to be an exaggeration. The infantry comprised a captain, lieutenant, three ensigns, a drummer and one hundred musketeers. The cavalry consisted, in addition to Sir John Digby the garrison commander, Major Brookbanck, two captains, a lieutenant, two quartermasters, two corporals, eighty troopers and a reformado ensign. There were also a number of non-combatants who included Henry Ratcliffe and Archdeacon Beeley, parson Crompton and Thomas Bunning, chaplain to Lady Crane. One report also claims that '600 Armes, 6 peeces of Ordnance, and 80 brave horses' were taken at Grafton.

Aftermath

When the parliamentarian soldiers entered the house 'they found great and rich plunder'. Pillage was seen as the right of soldiers forced to storm a garrison and so it is not surprising to find that there were in the

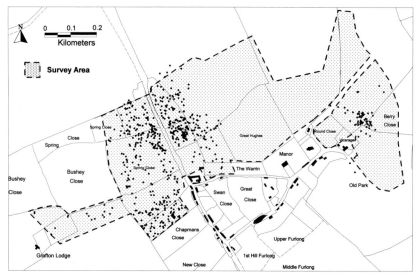

21 Civil War finds at Grafton Regis. The large number of musket balls recovered from the siege shows the ferocity of the engagement.

house 'many other things of great worth and estimation, which the common Souldiers divided amongst themselves'. It is said that there were 'many thousand pounds worth of goods taken, much plate and money, and good horse'. After the war Lady Crane's losses in the siege were estimated at over £5,000. By far the greatest loss was of course Grafton House itself, which as the parliamentary survey of 1650 explains 'was by the Parliaments Forces demollished and the Materialls that remaine are not considerable'. It had been fired by the parliamentary troops on Christmas Day and by 1650 all that remained of the once great house built by Henry VIII were the outbuildings: 'a brewhouse, kitchen and buttery with two chambers above and lofts over them, together with a stable of two bays, some other outhouses with two courtyards and a large, well planted orchard'.

According to one account, 'the soldiers had greate store of plate there, the booty did soe incourage them that they were very willing to fall upon Toster ... '. Towcester would indeed have been the sensible next target 'but the reason why they fell not upon it was because they were almost tyred out by reason of their hard quarter'. The garrison at Towcester was also far stronger than Grafton, one account claiming, perhaps rather implausibly, that it was so strong that 'an Army of ten thousand men in the summer are like to find a long pull of that town ... '. More important perhaps, the weather was too bad for a prolonged siege and Skippon probably expected that a relief force would be dispatched from Oxford, as indeed was the case. So on Christmas morning, before dawn, the besieging troops set fire to the huts they had built in the field and, rather than moving against Towcester, were withdrawn to their own garrisons. But before the army departed, following the common practice of both sides in the war, Grafton House itself was burnt down to prevent it being used again as a garrison. The march to Newport was a tiring one, 'by reason of the foulnesse of the weather and deepenesse of the way', despite its short distance, with the more important prisoners being sent on to London. Sir John Digby was committed to the Tower.

Skippon's withdrawal of his troops to their garrisons proved to be the right decision. Following the fall of Grafton the royalist forces at Brackley, Buckingham and thereabouts were withdrawn to Oxford, while the expectation of an assault was enough to dispose of the Towcester garrison. By 18 January 1644 they too had retreated towards Oxford. Later that spring the last of the royalist garrisons set up in the autumn offensive, at Hillesden near Buckingham, was also taken by storm by parliamentarian troops and the status quo restored. Unlike Newport Pagnell, where Skippon had garrisoned and re-fortified the town after the royalist withdrawal, there was no case and no resources to justify the maintenance of a garrison at Towcester. Instead the local people, from Stoke Bruerne and presumably from many other nearby villages, were drafted in to slight the defences.

For more than two years the royalists continued to hold sway over the south-west part of Northamptonshire, from their well-fortified garrison in Banbury castle. However, although they might occasionally plunder and skirmish as far north as Northampton, after the fall of Grafton, the royalists never again established a garrison in Northamptonshire.

The Commonwealth

The decline in royalist fortunes following the siege led to the dispersal of part of the Crown estate. In 1644 Sir George Strode of Westerham (Kent) and Arthur Duck of Chiswick, a master of the Court of Requests, purchased Grafton Park for £2,000 and £5,000 respectively. Lord Monson, who had taken the lease of the woodland, was later accused of cutting down all the trees in Pury Park and the greater part of those in Grafton for his own use, timber with an estimated value of £6,400. In addition he had ploughed up 100 acres. As early as 1649 there were said to be only 200 deer in the two parks combined.

Some building was carried out in Grafton in the aftermath of the Civil War. Tudor Cottage, at the south-west corner of the village, on the

Northampton road, is one of the best preserved small houses of this period in Northamptonshire, an example of the continuing drift of the village from its original core across the main road, undoubtedly drawn by the opportunities provided by traffic on what was one of the major roads in England. The datestone of 1653 has a fleur-de-lys flanked by roses. The cottage is built of coursed, squared limestone with a thatched roof. However, some of the internal architectural features date back to the 16th century, in particular the stone doorway on the left wall, now in the interior owing to later extensions, the winder stairway, and the stone fireplace upstairs with a moulded Tudor-arched head and cut spandrels.

CHARLES II
AND THE LATER
SEVENTEENTH CENTURY

After Charles II's Restoration in 1660, royal officials faced the complicated task of resolving conflicting claims to the various parts of the honor of Grafton which had been alienated by Charles I. At Grafton Regis itself the estate was split into two parts: the Crown retained the land around the village, while Grafton Park to the west remained with the heirs of Sir George Strode and Arthur Duck.

The 1st Duke of Grafton

Despite the loss of Grafton Park and other lands the honor of Grafton remained a valuable gift. It was given to Charles's Queen, Catherine of Braganza, in 1665. In 1673, when Catherine had failed to produce an heir, a reversionary grant was made to Charles's minister and leading member of the Cabal, Henry Bennet, Earl of Arlington, who donated a handsome silver-gilt chalice to the church at Grafton. The grant was made with remainder to Charles II's son Henry FitzRoy by his mistress Barbara Villiers, Countess of Castlemaine and later Duchess of Cleveland, one of the great beauties of the Restoration era. Charles made the grant 'in consideration of natural love and affection to his natural son'. He also arranged for Henry to marry Arlington's daughter and heiress Isabella. In 1675 Henry was created Duke of Grafton by the King. He was, perhaps, the most able of all Charles II's children, described by the diarist John Evelyn as 'rudely bred, but exceeding handsome, far exceeding any other of the king's natural issue'. The Duke was appointed colonel of the First Foot Guards, Vice-Admiral of England and Knight of the Garter. A close associate of John Churchill, the future Duke of Marlborough, he was killed tragically young at the age of 27 leading his troops ashore at the siege of Cork in 1690. His descendants have continued to hold land surrounding the village to the present day.

22 Charles II by Sir Peter Lely. The King created his natural son Henry FitzRoy Duke of Grafton.

The Manor

With the upsurge of confidence and prosperity following the Restoration, Marthana Wilson, as executrix of Dame Mary Crane, was petitioning in 1661 (unsuccessfully, as it proved) for a lease of a house built on part of the site of the mansion demolished only eighteen years before. This was presumably the oldest part of the existing building, which is shown in elevation on Collier and Baker's plan of Grafton of 1725 as an E-plan mansion of 2½ storeys with a central doorway. There is a local tradition that the house incorporates two of the walls of the mansion demolished in 1643 but this has never been firmly established. Collier and Baker show only one outbuilding to the south-east of the house (where an extensive range of farm buildings later grew up). This is clearly the range fronting the lane near the churchyard whose north wall is lit by Tudor mullioned windows and whose south wall has a buttress of similar date, which has been identified as the 'offices along the street side', the only recognisable surviving part of Henry VIII's mansion.

The Crown Estate

Despite the destruction of the siege, and the consequent need for rebuilding, the organisation of the manor had changed little since the 1540s. In a survey of 1660 the enclosed pastures (the former Church Field, Mill Field, Twyford Field and Twycross Field to the north of the village, plus the Old Park to the south), amounting in all to 467 acres, together with 119 acres of meadow, continued to be leased to William Downhall, an absentee courtier who was the executor of Sir Robert Osborne. The remaining 238 acres of arable and 12 acres of meadow were let to five people, who had about 47 acres each.

Little attempt was made to exploit the full commercial value of the estate. When the lease of the demesnes of 1610 finally expired in 1663, the land was let at twice the old figure of £42 12s. 11d. p.a., which had remained unchanged since the mid 16th century. At the same date the five farms were let for between 21s. and 43s. p.a., and three smaller holdings at between 10s. and 26s. p.a., so that the entire estate produced only £53 18s. 10d. p.a., against a far greater estimated value of £669 15s. 8d. Queen Catherine's trustees continued the same policy after 1665, granting 21-year leases at unchanged rents, combined with entry fines.

23 Barbara Villiers, Duchess of Cleveland, by Sir Peter Lely. The 1st Duke of Grafton's mother was Charles II's glamorous mistress, Barbara Villiers.

The Village

During this period there were five farmsteads in the village. Four of the farmhouses had a hall, parlour, buttery and kitchen downstairs (the fifth lacked a buttery), with three or four chambers over, and between five and 11 bays of stabling and barns, as well as other buildings, in the yard. The King's Arms similarly had a hall, parlour and kitchen, with a cellar beneath the parlour and four chambers, as well as nine bays of stabling and a five-bay barn. The inn was obviously an important building, since it was normally the meeting place of of the manor court, held twice a year by the lord's steward to deal with farming matters and minor offences such as the blocking of watercourses or grazing too many animals on the common land of the manor. The inn was one of five alehouses listed in 1673, the number dropping to four in the following year, although no more than one of them may have been in use as an inn at any one time. The largest cottage in the village had cellars, a seven-bay malting house and five bays of stabling, which suggests it had once been an inn. The 'inn at Grafton' was among the premises Sir Miles Fleetwood sought as recompense for his losses in trying to recover Grafton House for the King.

Elsewhere in the village there was a three-bay single-storey smithy. There were six cottages erected on the manorial waste and another cottage with hall and parlour downstairs and two chambers over. Three other 'cottages' were comparable in size to the farmhouses, with three or four rooms downstairs and either three, four or five chambers. The 1660 survey lists eleven cottages in the village, all said to have been built on the waste, mostly with half an acre of land each. The remaining 300 acres of the parish lay within the Grafton Park estate.

Grafton Park

Grafton Park, amounting in total to 1,020 acres in Grafton and neighbouring parishes, had passed into different ownership. Sir George Strode and the heirs of Arthur Duck who had purchased the land in 1644 complained that they had been prevented from enjoying it by the 'late troubles', and that the parks and woods were now wasted. By 1660 Ferdinand Marsham was tenant of the estate, which had allegedly been damaged by Lord Monson. The position of Grafton Park was further complicated by the title to the £7,000 cost of purchase changing hands. After a protracted dispute between the heirs of Strode and Duck, the estate devolved to William Harbord, whose wife Mary was Duck's

24 Henry, 1st Duke of Grafton KG, by Thomas Hawker. The 1st Duke was probably the most able of Charles II's children. A fine soldier and sailor before his early death at the age of 27.

daughter. Although the Crown made an offer of £9,000 for the purchase of the two parks, this came to nothing and they remained in Harbord's possession.

Whether or not Charles II resented this diminution of the Crown estate, Harbord soon fell into royal disfavour. The political situation was very unstable, with the country polarised between Whigs and Tories. In the summer of 1683, the disgruntled Whigs, who had been defeated in their attempt to exclude Charles II's brother James from the succession, tried to assassinate the King. In an atmosphere of fear and suspicion following the discovery of the Rye House Plot, in July Harbord's house at Grafton Park was searched for arms, of which some were found hidden beneath dirty linen in a maid's room. Harbord complained angrily to both the Lord-Lieutenant and the Secretary of State that the militia officer in charge had used excessive force and bad language, and had ransacked the house. He also claimed that the weapons found were merely sporting guns and that he needed to keep arms at his home, which was encompassed by two great roads and a forest, since he had been the target of two attempted robberies within the last year. The Secretary of State ordered enquiries to be made and that in the meantime Harbord's weapons should be returned. In August Harbord strongly reiterated his version of events and refuted imputations concerning his loyalty to the Crown. Others persisted in their allegations that Harbord was not to be trusted, pointing out that he had travelled to both Bath and Oxford excessively armed and escorted, as the whole county had noticed. Early in September the Lord-Lieutenant was still resisting pressure from the Secretary of State to return Harbord's arms and defending his officers against complaints concerning a third search of his house. Nothing more was heard of the matter. In 1691, when the Whigs had gained power under William and Mary, Harbord was appointed ambassador to Turkey to mediate between the Sultan and the Emperor Leopold, but died on his way at Belgrade in July 1692. In his will, made the previous November, he divided all his freehold estate equally between his four daughters.

THE EIGHTEENTH CENTURY

During the 18th century the village of Grafton Regis remained chiefly an agricultural community, mostly under the control of the Grafton estate. However, with the development of the turnpike road and the Grand Junction Canal there was a growth of different trades which prefigures the way in which the Industrial Revolution would transform English society in the 19th century. Much of the fascination of Grafton Regis during this period lies in the extraordinarily complete records of the Grafton estate, particularly under the enlightened ownership of the 2nd Duke of Grafton. These provide an excellent example of the way in which the wealth and power of the great Whig magnates, who ruled England throughout the century, was based on the careful management of their landed estates.

At the beginning of the century Grafton Manor, known as the Great House, was inhabited by the widow of the 1st Duke of Grafton and her second husband Sir Thomas Hanmer, although they spent most of their time in London. Duchess Isabella's account book (1707–22) is very revealing of her fashionable lifestyle. Numerous entries to her staymaker, French couturier and shoemaker, together with outings to the theatre and opera, are interspersed with more prosaic demands for toothache plasters. In a similar vein she balanced her heavy losses at cards, sometimes as much as £10 in a month, as well as occasional bets on the lottery, with frequent donations to the poor and the sick, including a blind man at the door, a mad captain, a man with dancing dogs and a poor woman at the church gate. With such a hectic social life in London, the Duchess had little time to devote to Grafton Regis. She and her husband showed little desire to change the antiquated system at Grafton of 21-year leases at unchanged rents combined with entry fines.

The Grafton Survey of 1725

Her son the 2nd Duke, however, who owned the honor, determined on a radically new approach to the management of his land. A major figure at Court, Knight of the Garter, Viceroy of Ireland and Lord Chamberlain for 33 years, he chose to make Wakefield Lodge, a few miles away to the south-west, which he acquired as hereditary ranger of Whittlewood

71

Forest, his Northamptonshire seat. The Duke commissioned William Kent to build a magnificent classical house and lay out a park with an ornamental lake. Wakefield Lodge, home of the Grafton Hunt, founded in the mid 18th century, was to be the base from which the estate would continue to be administered until the sales of 1919–20. On the death of Duchess Isabella and Hanmer in the early 1720s, the Duke decided to introduce a new system. In 1724 he appointed a body of commissioners to advise him on the running of the estate. Their policy was to lay down an increasing proportion of Grafton to permanent pasture. Bridges, writing about 1720, was clearly referring to this when he described Grafton as an 'inclosed lordship, famous for its meadow grounds and pastures'.

An up-to-date survey of the whole estate was commissioned from Joseph Collier and William Baker. This was remarkably detailed, accompanied by maps, and encompasses all the Duke's Northamptonshire estate, extending from Greens Norton to Potterspury. The commissioners' minutes show them engaged in various aspects of farm management, undertaking building works, making valuations, drawing up new leases etc. It also describes the enclosure of the remaining part of Grafton's open fields. From the similarity of the acreages of the old enclosures and the open-field land, it is clear that the landscape of 1725 (see Fig. 27) was much the same as that described in summary form in 1660.

In 1725 the enclosed land was let to George Stokes, who lived at the manor house. He tenanted 608 acres, lying mostly to the north of the village. Each close is named in the survey, giving the acreage. The map shows that many closes were larger than the modern fields. The survey continues with the village houses and paddocks, each of which are numbered and keyed to the plan. The parsonage house and adjacent close was six acres and there were over nine acres of glebe scattered in the common fields. Only four other people had land in the open fields, which totalled 257 acres of ridge and furrow with additional meadow and common. These fields were known as Sties Field to the west of the main road, Upper Field closest to the village, and Fenn and Bancroft Fields between the main road, the Yardley parish boundary and the river (before enclosure they were known as Hill Field, Fenn Field and Low Field). To the west lay Dunmore Meadow, the detached portion of Alderton parish, and Leach Meadow. The 1725 survey gives the name Park to a close south of the church, which was probably a medieval manorial enclosure.

By 1721 the central part of Grafton Park still had coppices and was stocked with deer, but some of the closes outside were arable. A survey

25 Isabella, wife of the 1st Duke of Grafton, and her son Charles, later 2nd Duke of Grafton. Part of Isabella's long widowhood was spent at Grafton Manor.

lists the name of the tenant of each close, giving its acreage, use and rent. The Old Park and coppices added up to 179 acres and the total area of the main park amounted to 963 acres. The plan marks deer on the lawn, and names several of the coppices. By the 1830s much of the park was arable but an old inhabitant remembered the paling reaching almost to the village.

At the end of the 1725 survey the open fields are described in detail, taking each of the great fields in order and then each furlong, listing the number of land ridges in every parcel, the owner, the tenant, the length and breadth in links (100 links = 1 chain (22 yards)) and the area in acres, roods and poles. The meadow is similarly described in strips, but it was never ploughed or ridged up, the strips being marked out annually before they were mowed for hay and then thrown open to common grazing. The surveyors were paid 6d. per acre for their work until March 1727, when they said they could not continue at that price because of 'the great trouble in measuring the common fields it lying in such small parcels'. It was recommended to give them 8d. per acre for 'what has been done and for what is to be done', and the Duke agreed.

One of the purposes of the 1725 survey was to provide information to value the land and enclose it, a relatively easy matter as the Duke owned it all except for the 9 acres of glebe and 2½ acres of charity land. The field-book was studied at Wakefield Lodge in September 1726 and the data rearranged into areas of grass and arable (because they were priced differently). As well as 272 acres of common field, there were 45 acres of cow common, 4 acres of enclosed meadow belonging to the rectory, and assorted pockets of waste and other land. The rector had to be compensated for his land, for his right to put two cows on the commons, and for tithes. The subsequent agreement between the Duke of Grafton on one side and the Bishop of Peterborough, rector and churchwardens on the other was confirmed by a private Act of Parliament of 1727, the first to be obtained in connection with enclosure in Northamptonshire.

The Grafton Estate under the 2nd Duke

In the winter of 1727–8 the commissioners set to work. The commission determined policy both in general and in matters of detail, and gave instructions to officials on the spot. Shorter leases at rack rents replaced the previous system of granting 21-year leases at low rents. In January 1728 the commissioners ordered that the common fields of Grafton be divided one from another with a new ditch and bank and a double layer

26 Charles, 2nd Duke of Grafton KG, by Sir Joshua Reynolds PRA. The Duke created a model estate and there are full records of the changes he introduced at Grafton in the early 18th century.

of whitethorn quick, and two sets of ash, oak, or elm to be planted every 220 yards. There were precise instructions to set quick in the top sod and throw clay 'and other stuff' out of the ditch bottom behind the bank. Wood for fencing was to be obtained from coppices elsewhere on the Grafton estate due for cutting that year. In September a local carpenter was being asked to estimate the cost of post and rail fencing along the boundary between Grafton and Yardley Gobion. The new enclosures, or fields as we would now call them, were still sown with arable crops in

Grafton Enclosed Field Names in 1721–25

See map opposite

1725   **1721**

No	Name	Ac.	
1	Dunmoor Mead	13	p
2	Leach Mead	20	p
3	Lamb Ground	27	p
4	Great Galhouse Mead	13	p
5	Little Galhouse Mead	6	p
6	Holman's Ground	28	p
7	Twyford Ground	73	p
8	Great Church Field	73	p
9	Middle Church Field	87	p
10	Mill Field	107	p
11	Millmead	10	p
12	Bosenham Mead	33	p
13	Parsonage Close	6	p
14	The Dean	30	p
15	Shittam	6	p
16	Berry Close	10	p
17	Old Park	34	p
18	Fen Close	14	p
19	Great Hughs	12	p
20	Little Hughs	3	p
21	Great Warren	3	p
22	Good Close	–	p
23	Swan Close	–	p

No	Name	Ac.	
30	Spring Close	10	p
31	Chapmans Close	5	m
32	Forster Close	9	m
33	Upper New Close	8	m
34	Middle New Close	8	m
35	Lower New Close	5	m
36	Upper New Close	16	p
37	Stone Pit Ground	20	a
38	Johnsons Ground		
39	and House Close	95	p
40	Bushy Close	14	m
41	Dudleys Close	17	p
42	Lodge Copse	42	m
43	Grafton Park	179	pw
44	Great Pondhill	19	a
45	Spring Close Copse	3	w
46	Spring Close	3	p
47	Spring Close	4	m
48	Bushy Close	11	a
49	Dawks Close	13	p
50	Willow Close	10	m
51	Toddy Close	14	a
52	Bushy Close	12	a
53	Paddocks	14	p
54	Dry Leys	8	a
55	Little Pond Hill	17	a
56	Horse Close	18	p
57	Great Owls Moor	24	mp
58	Lyons Wood	28	p
59	Plumb Park	11	p
60	Plumb Park	8	p
61	Plumb Park	11	p
62	Foxholes	22	p

Key to right-hand column: a = arable, m = meadow, p = pasture, w = wood

Source: Northants. Record Office, YZ 8943 (1721) and G 1635 (1725).

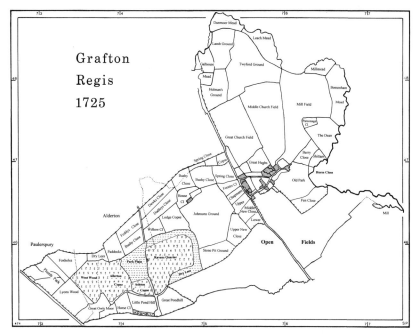

27 Grafton field names after enclosure. Names in the park are from a survey of 1721, the remainder from one of 1725.

1729 and not immediately laid down to pasture.

Despite their power in the locality, where the Duke of Grafton owned perhaps 15,000 acres, it is interesting to note how each and every transaction was open to extensive negotiation. The rector had successfully insisted that the commissioners treat with the bishop before enclosing his land. Eventually, he was offered £53 p.a. Much time was spent trying to induce tenants of the manor to allow the cow commons to be planted with corn for three seasons before being laid down with grass seed. The commissioners were unable to obtain more than £45 p.a., whereas they wanted £50. The churchwardens were paid 20s. for 2½ acres held for charitable purposes.

The tenants proved equally tricky. John Newman gave notice that he wished to give up his farm at Lady Day 1728 and subsequently left owing rent; and Alice Foster, the tenant of the largest of the old open-field farms, died intestate in the summer of 1727. In September of the same year the commissioners opened negotiations with the two remaining tenants, Thomas Smith and Elizabeth Finall (who appears to have succeeded to Mrs Foster's tenancy), initially to see if each would take half the newly enclosed land. When they refused to accept the estate's terms, the commissioners implemented a decision taken earlier in the year, when the existing tenants were given six months' notice to quit at Michaelmas 1729, and the estate was taken in hand from the latter date.

The large number of crops the commissioners planted during 1730–1 showed their desire to experiment, the care taken to gain maximum yields from the soil, and their willingness to change their plans. Upper, Fen and Bancroft fields were sown with a mixture of barley, trefoil, hayseed, rye grass, oats, beans and clover. Ten acres in the driest part of Sties Field was to be sown with turnips and the whole field fallowed the following summer. The commissioners also agreed that some of their number should go down to Grafton to direct the ploughing and sowing and to find a competent man to supervise the work.

Decisions on the crops and livestock changed from month to month. The cow commons proved particularly problematic. When no tenant to take the grazing was forthcoming, William Sherd, the Duke's steward at Wakefield Lodge, considered Scotch or Welsh bullocks and wethers (castrated rams), and lambs from the Duke's Suffolk estate at Euston, before settling for joist cattle instead. The commissioners seem to have been constantly surprised by the wetness of the ground. Although Collier had made drains to run off water, the weather had been so wet that Bancroft and Sties fields were left fallow. Upper and Fen fields, however, were sown and well laid down. In September 1730 the commissioners rode over the former common fields to inspect the fallows and the progress of the grass seeds sown in the spring. They found the fallows in Bancroft and Sties fields well ploughed, and the clover in Upper and Fen fields coming on well, but the hay seed had made little progress.

The Duke's commissioners kept the arable at Grafton in hand for only two seasons and in September 1731 granted two nine-year leases of the estate. William Wayte of Blakesley took a holding of 156 acres made up of Upper, Bancroft and Fen fields, plus the meadow at Yardley Mill Holme (which lay just inside Potterspury parish in Yardley common field), together with the farmhouse near the junction of the two lanes in Grafton previously occupied by Thomas Smith, for a rent of £144 p.a. The land to the west of the main road (the old Sties Field), together with the cow commons, making a total of 175 acres, was leased at £112 p.a. to John Lloyd of Pattishall, who had the house at the corner of Church Lane and Northampton Road previously occupied by William Finall. The three farms at Grafton, together with the parsonage (for which the rector was paying a rent of £2 10s. p.a. since enclosure), an eight-acre smallholding at the corner of the lane leading up to the manor, and 18 cottages, in all some 970 acres, were thus producing a total rent of £872 15s. p.a. in the 1730s. This was a substantial increase on the figure achieved immediately before enclosure, especially bearing in mind that two-thirds of the total came from the lease of the demesnes, which could not be raised at enclosure. The former common field land was producing almost £300 a year, compared with less than £150 when it was briefly let at a rack rent in 1726, and vastly more than the sum received when the Duke took control of the estate in 1723.

The estate's preference for enclosure is reflected in its dealings with its tenants. The leases to William Wayte and John Lloyd in 1731 required them not to plough more than one-third of their land at any one time, nor to take more than two crops without fallowing or laying down the land with grass seed, and when both farms were surveyed a few years later it was noted that if both were sown with natural grass seed the value of the land would increase to that of George Stokes's pasture. Samuel Gallard of Muscot succeeded Leonard Lloyd at the farm created out of the old Sties Field let to John Lloyd in 1731, where he was granted a 15-year lease from Lady Day 1746 at £114 2s. p.a. on condition that he leave part of Sties Field next to the main road as pasture throughout his tenancy and plough up the rest of his holding, but only a third at a time. On Lady Day 1737 George Stokes gave up most of the former demesne pastures, retaining only the mansion and land worth £60 p.a.; he died shortly afterwards.

Most of Stokes's estate, together with the farm previously held by the Wayte family, was leased in October 1739 for three years from the following Lady Day at £200 p.a. to John Clare of Shenley (Bucks.), who was succeeded at his death by his brother James. In 1755 James Clare was granted a nine-year lease of the same estate at £210 p.a. for the first four years, £220 p.a. thereafter. The remaining 93 acres of Stokes's estate was in the hands of Edward Clarke by 1751, for which he was paying £88 p.a., a figure increased to £90 p.a. when he was replaced by Joseph Smith in 1755, who took an eight-year lease of the same acreage. The term was evidently chosen to expire at the same time as a twelve-year lease granted to Smith in 1751 of the farmhouse on the main road known as the Blackmoors Head which had once formed part of George Stokes's estate.

The scope for bringing the land south of the village up to the same standard as the pastures to the north was mentioned again after James Clare succeeded the Waytes in 1751, although it was noted that grazing was difficult to let, because of the continuance of distemper among horned cattle, then prevalent within a few miles of Grafton. On the other hand, when John Warr took the Great House farm in 1753 and Joseph Smith the land at Twyford Meadow and Leach Meadow two years later, both leases contained a covenant restraining the tenants from ploughing any of the existing pasture and meadow. James Clare also agreed in

1755, only to plough the Upper Field and that part of Bancroft Field which had for many years been in tillage, not to take more than two corn crops without a summer fallowing, and not to plough enclosed pasture or meadow.

The Grafton Estate under the 3rd Duke

The results of this policy can be seen in the survey taken after the death of the 2nd Duke in 1757. His grandson, the 3rd Duke, had the whole Wakefield Lodge estate surveyed afresh on succeeding to the title. Augustus Henry FitzRoy was a leading Whig politician, the protégé of Pitt the Elder, and successively Secretary of State and a Lord of the Treasury before becoming Prime Minister between 1767 and 1770. He was a strong advocate of a conciliatory policy towards the American colonies. The Duke was later to become Chancellor of Cambridge University. As Chambers' *Biographical Dictionary* judiciously comments: 'Though possessed of more honesty of purpose than the invectives of Junius would have us believe, he had a weakness for the fair sex and for the turf which often distracted him from more urgent business'.

Despite these distractions, the 3rd Duke continued his predecessor's enlightened and careful management of the Grafton estates. The survey lists the property of each tenant, its value per acre and the total rent, and has interesting comments on the tenants and what should be done when leases fell due for renewal. It uses the same numbers for the houses and the field acreages as the 1725 survey. Fen and Bancroft fields were noted to be 'annually improving and in a few years will be the best pasture in the parish'. Half of Sties Field was also said to be good pasture, continually improving. The houses and farm buildings on the manor were in good repair and the holdings generally let at full rent, with the only scope for increases coming from the creation of more permanent pasture. By this date some of the large pieces had been subdivided, hence the 87 acres of Middle Church Field were let in three parts. The old open-field land was scarcely used as arable. Only a few acres were to be laid down when the lease expired. Continued subdivision occurred until the field pattern recorded on the Ordnance Survey in 1884 was achieved (probably by about 1820). Recent hedge removal has produced the present-day fields.

Under the new Duke's management, Grafton was divided between four farms let at between £114 2s. and £240 p.a., one smaller holding (£31 p.a.), a parcel of accommodation land (£57 2s.), the parsonage, where the rector continued to pay rent of £2 10s. p.a., and a dozen

28 Augustus Henry, 3rd Duke of Grafton KG, by Nathaniel Dance RA. The 3rd Duke was one of the great Whig magnates of the 18th century. He was Prime Minister and Chancellor of Cambridge University.

cottages. The total rental for the manor was £775 p.a., about £100 below the figure achieved immediately after enclosure. Since rents on the other farms had generally been edged up at each change of tenant, this reduction was entirely the result of the break-up of the old demesne pastures, where George Stokes's successors were together paying rather

29 The 3rd Duke of Grafton viewing his stud, by Thomas Rowlandson. The Duke had a passion for horses and racing and was a great patron of George Stubbs.

less than the £590 10s. p.a. specified in his lease of 1721.

On the third Duke's succession, the three largest tenants at Grafton had nine- or twelve-year leases, whereas the three smaller holdings were let at will, as were the cottages. By the end of the 18th century all the farms had been converted into tenancies at will and rents had been increased, so that the estate as a whole was producing £950 p.a., and the number of holdings slightly reduced. Neither during the third Duke's time (1757–1811) nor after his death was the estate at Grafton enlarged by purchase, as was the case in neighbouring parishes, apart from one acre in Dunmore Meadow in 1763.

James Clare's son William had been allowed to take over his father's farm in 1783 at the old rent of £122 p.a., on condition that the property would be kept neat and the boggy parts of the Old Park drained. When in 1800 the Duke found that neither condition had been met and that, apart from the house, the farm was still in a slovenly condition, he raised the rent to £245 p.a. from 1802 as an example to the other tenants, a rare case in the third Duke's time of a rent being increased other than when a tenancy changed hands. Clare died in 1804 and the Duke offered the farm, where the estate had built a new cow-house and repaired the homestead, to his son William, who was only 19, at £300 p.a. for two years, since 'I was desirous of giving him an opportunity of shewing if he possesses the requisite qualifications of a good Tenant'.

In the same way, when Samuel Gallard died in 1758, his son Thomas was offered the tenancy at £160 p.a. for three years, then £165 for another three and £170 thereafter, compared with the £128 his father had been paying, although in this case the estate had provided a new barn and other buildings, which had greatly improved the farm. The land previously let to John Willifer had also been added to the holding in 1785. By contrast, when Joseph Smith died in 1798, his nephew, also Joseph Smith, took over only part of his uncle's farm at £50 p.a., together with a cottage in the village at 30s. p.a., while the farmhouse and the rest of the land were let to John Pittam at £245 p.a.

The Manor

At the Great House, as the Manor was known in this period, George Stokes was succeeded after his death at first by William Bradford and later, in 1749, by Robert Millegan. Four years later John Warr took the house and 227 acres of land on a 12-year lease at £240 p.a. During this period the manor house had become a farmstead, although, according to the new tenant in 1749, not a very satisfactory one. As well as extensive repairs to the house itself, which was said to be cracked through in three places and the roof (on which jackdaws had spoiled the thatch) propped up in two, Millegan also wanted a number of new outbuildings erecting in the 'yard belonging to the Lower Tenement'. The latter, which had previously been used as stabling but was excluded from the premises being offered him, is likely to be the Tudor range near the road, since it stands in a yard several feet lower than the level of the main house. Millegan also asked for alterations to the house to create additional store-rooms and bedrooms, there being 'only three rooms above stairs in the Great House'. An inventory of dressers, drawers and shelves at the house, drawn up at the same time, mentions only a hall, kitchen and two chambers.

During John Warr's tenancy, the 'Lower Yard', which had been let separately, was included in the farm lease. By 1800 the Manor House, as it was called in a new survey made following the building of the Grand Junction Canal through the parish, was in the hands of Thomas Warr (John having died in 1784), who was paying £279 p.a., rather less than its revaluation at £300.

Grafton Park

Meanwhile, Grafton Park, which had been divided between the heirs of Strode and Duck, gradually came into the hands of John Sharp, the eldest son of the Archbishop of York. His marriage in March 1738 to the heiress Anna Maria Hosier of Wicken ensured his possession of the entire estate. Both Grafton Park and Wicken passed to Sharp's only daughter and heiress Elizabeth, the wife of Thomas Prowse. From her the estate passed in turn in 1802 to her second daughter Elizabeth, the wife of Sir John Mordaunt Bt. The Mordaunts were already sole owners in Wicken parish, a few miles to the south, which they had inherited from Mrs Prowse. They retained both estates for most of the 19th century.

In the 1830s Baker observed that both Grafton Park and Potterspury Park, once well stocked with deer and 'intersected by rectilinear avenues of noble oaks', had long been sacrificed to the cause of agricultural improvement and converted into farms. This process may have begun after the sale of 1644 and was clearly well advanced by the 1720s, when Bridges observed that the park 'hath long ago been converted into pasture and tillage'. The survey of 1721 shows that much of the Grafton and Alderton portion of Grafton Park had been disparked and enclosed, either as pasture or meadow. What appears to be the original nucleus of the park, amounting to about 180 acres, was still wooded and kept in hand by John Sharp. Despite the damage said to have been done by Lord Monson, there was also a considerable quantity of wood elsewhere on the estate in the 1720s, mostly oak, ash and small amounts of maple and crabtree. In addition to the 208 acres held by Sharp himself, the Grafton portion of the estate had one other large tenant in 1721, Stephen Webb, who had 144 acres in a consolidated block around Grafton Lodge, including 30 acres of arable, while the rest of the former park was divided into holdings of 30 acres or less.

The Village

Until modern times few residents of Grafton Regis followed occupations other than farming. The five farmsteads in the village in the 16th and 17th centuries had been reduced to two by 1731 and thereafter there were never more than four. In addition, there was a handsome red brick parsonage to the east of the church and a growing number of cottages with small pieces of land attached, mostly built on the waste on either side of the main road between the two junctions. The number of cottages had risen from eleven in 1660 to about 20 in 1725. Probably by the middle of the 18th century (and certainly by 1800) the farmhouses were all stone-built with tiled roofs, although in 1749 the Great House was apparently still thatched, as were most of the cottages.

There is no mill site in the parish and references to 'Grafton Mill' refer to Bozenham Mill, which lies just inside Hartwell, to which the farmers of Grafton evidently took their corn. One of the buildings on the west side of the main road marked on Collier and Baker's plan of 1725 is identified in the estate survey of 1757 as a cottage and smithy, said then to be in bad repair. Among other tradesmen normally found in a village the size of Grafton, a carpenter named John Dawson died there in 1783 and Thomas Dawson was described as 'tailor and shopkeeper' at his death in 1815.

The life of Thomas Smith, a labourer and parish clerk of Grafton, gives an idea of how hard life could be in the 18th century. Smith was baptised in Grafton in 1727 and married Susannah in 1770. They produced eight children between 1771 and 1792. He worked on the turnpike road between Grafton Regis and Stoke Bruerne, often at Twyford Bridge, where the tollgate was installed, until his death in 1795, regularly digging loads of stone and gravel for 8d. a yard, earning himself 1s. a day. From this small income, Smith rented a cottage at Grafton for 7s. p.a. Working on the turnpike became a family occupation, and Smith's sons William, Samuel and James all worked on the road. During the 19th century the turnpike gradually declined with competition from the Grand Junction Canal and later the railway.

As one would expect in a village which stands on a major road, there had been four or five houses licensed as inns or alehouses since the 17th century. In the 1720s the farmhouse at the junction on the main road at the northern end of the village was called the 'Blackmoor's Head', presumably indicating that it had previously been an inn. It was then one of several houses in the village leased to Alice Foster, but was occupied by a man named Finall, possibly the Henry Finall who was described as an innholder when he died in 1730. At this period Grafton's inn was the Bull, which stood on the same side of the road at the opposite end of the village, on the corner of the main road and Church Lane. In 1726 the landlord there was John Feary but the premises were held on a Crown lease (which did not expire until 1737) by Thomas Foster, whose family had been lessees since 1587. By 1757 the Fosters' house had become a farmstead, occupied by Samuel Gallard, and in its place the cottage immediately to the north, where another old Crown lease had expired in 1729, had become an alehouse, tenanted by Widow Dawson.

The Court

During the first half of the 18th century the manor court at Grafton retained something of its status as the principal court for the honor, with residual jurisdiction over several townships in which the Wakefield Lodge estate owned little, if any, land. The court was also responsible for the appointment of officials known as petty constables, haywards (officers in charge of fences and enclosures), field keepers, headboroughs and thirdboroughs (assistant constables) for Wicken and Bugbrooke in the early 18th century. There are also records of jurors attending on behalf of Hartwell, Roade, Wicken, Hanslope and Bugbrooke.

The court sat at Grafton in April and October each year in the first half of the century, transacting both leet and baron business for Grafton, Hartwell and Roade, and occasionally the other townships represented on the jury. For Grafton itself leet business disappeared entirely after enclosure: the last orders for stopping up gaps in the common fields or stinting the commons were made at the court held in April 1729, whereas for Roade and Hartwell (where the open fields were not enclosed until 1819 and 1828 respectively) a full range of farming business continued to be transacted. Most of the baron business was also concerned with changes in ownership in Roade and Hartwell, rather than Grafton.

By the 1760s the court at Grafton, like those for the rest of the Wakefield Lodge estate, was sitting only once a year, at the end of April or the beginning of May, and after 1775 sat only in alternate years. By the end of the century there was almost no business coming before the court at Grafton. Also in the 1770s the small size of the two parishes of Alderton and Grafton led to their being combined into a single church living, with Alderton rectory being annexed to that of Grafton.

The Canal

Apart from enclosure, the other major change in the topography of Grafton Regis in the 18th century was the building of the Grand Junction Canal in the 1790s, the greatest civil engineering undertaking in England. It was to be twice as wide as the existing Oxford Canal. One of its major backers was the 3rd Duke of Grafton, and the canal was routed through his land in south Northamptonshire, including the section running past Grafton Regis. Entering the parish just to the east of Stone Bridge, the canal ran due north through the old Bancroft Field and Fenn Field and then closely followed the Tove to Dunmore Meadow, where it was supplied with water from the river before continuing north into Stoke Bruerne parish. There were no locks on the stretch in Grafton and the nearest wharf was at Yardley, a little over a mile from the village, although four bridges were built to provide access to fields severed by the canal. The Duke was anxious to complete the work quickly as his tenants were complaining about the canal labourers. It was opened in 1800.

One of these bridges carried a new lane built from the cottages to the north of the church through the enclosed pastures to Bozenham Mill; before this period the lane which ran past the church petered out at the cottages just beyond and the only access to the mill was via the lane which ran from the main road at the Alderton turning due east across the fields. This provided a convenient route for the farmers of Alderton but was a long way round for their neighbours in Grafton. A bridge over the canal was provided to preserve this means of access, which was still in use as a footpath in the late 19th century but has since been abandoned in favour of the lane from Grafton village to the mill.

THE NINETEENTH CENTURY

The history of Grafton Regis in the 19th century, as reflected in the census of 1851, shows the increasing diversity of the village. Although the majority of men continued to be employed on the land, most as agricultural labourers, with the occasional shepherd, groom, and ratcatcher, and almost all their wives worked as lacemakers or servants, there are records of a number of other trades. Robert Warr is entered as a victualler, John Smith as a carpenter, James Baldwin as a tailor, Joshua Dawson as a lace merchant, Thomas Smith as a butcher and Joseph Garrat as a shoe manufacturer. Thirty years later, the census records Mary Ann Atkins as shop keeper, Edwin Webb as innkeeper and the whole family of Thomas Blunt employed as beehive makers. By now Grafton contained a newly established school and a Nonconformist meeting. This diversity reflects the growing complexity of Victorian society even in rural communities.

The stories recounted on the tombs of villagers buried in the churchyard show how hard life could be. Infant mortality continued to be high despite the advances in medicine. Three children in the Blunt family died of scarlet fever at the beginning of February 1838. The same year two members of the Dawson family died of smallpox and Jemima Morton was struck down by typhus. 1867 was another bad year in the history of the village, with Jane and Lucy Atkins, and Annis Lyman all dying in childbirth. New technology could also be fatally dangerous. George Baldwin and John Addington were both killed on the new railroad in June 1837.

The Manor

In 1833 Captain (later Colonel) George FitzRoy of the Grenadier Guards, a grandson of the third Duke, decided to make his home at the Manor House, which had been modernised by the tenant George Seabrooke some three years previously. He was elder brother of Robert FitzRoy, captain of the *Beagle*, in which Darwin made his momentous voyage round the world, the basis for his famous work *The Origin of Species*. FitzRoy established himself as a gentleman farmer of some 367 acres. He remained until his death in 1883, when he was succeeded by his son,

30 Charlotte Maria, Countess of Euston, by John Hoppner RA. A memorial by John Flaxman to Charlotte Maria is the most beautiful of the later monuments in the church of St Mary the Virgin.

Major-General George Robert FitzRoy of the Coldstream Guards, who continued to farm at Grafton until 1899. The village thus acquired a resident squire for the first time in its modern history, admittedly only a tenant but at the same time a member of the family that owned most of the parish. The FitzRoys were not only by some way the largest farmers in the village, but the general in particular involved himself in the life of the community, serving as a school manager and as a rural district councillor. At the Manor, despite the rent reductions of the 1880s,

General FitzRoy gave notice in February 1895 to quit at Lady Day the following year, complaining to the Duke's agent that he could not 'afford to lose the large sums I do yearly on my farm any longer'. He claimed that he had lost a total of £1,390 since he took over the farm from his father, all but £198 of that sum since 1890. He was, however, prepared to keep the farm if the rent was reduced to £274 p.a. from the £348 he had been paying up to that date. He clearly did not wish to leave if possible and in September 1895 accepted the Duke's 'final offer' of £300 p.a. from Lady Day 1896. When Henry John Conant took the Manor in 1899, with the same acreage as General FitzRoy had farmed, the estate was able to secure £400 p.a. in return for a 21-year lease, although only after agreeing to a lengthy list of repairs, which also led to a protracted dispute with Conant.

The FitzRoy Family and the Church

The affection in which the FitzRoys held the village can be seen in numerous memorials in the church. Both the colonel and the general are buried in the churchyard, and there is a memorial to the former under the belltower, and to his wife Louisa behind the lectern. The most beautiful memorial, however, on the south wall of the nave, commemorates the colonel's cousin Charlotte Maria, Countess of Euston, second daughter of the Earl of Waldegrave, 'whose virtues rendered her the object of the tenderest affection during life and afford the most consoling hopes of her eternal happiness to her surviving husband, by whom this monument is erected'. The simple design of the monument, flanked by the figures of Faith and Hope, by the great neo-classical sculptor John Flaxman, is especially fine. She was buried in the church on 8 February 1808 and there is a strong family tradition that she lived in the village. Beside her is a touching memorial by the sculptor William Behnes to her son James FitzRoy 'whose life was but a span'.

Scattered along the walls of the nave and the aisles are monuments to other members of the family, who took part in so many stirring events of British history and testify to the world-wide extent of the British Empire in the 19th century. Some of them were soldiers: Lord Charles FitzRoy, second son of the 4th Duke, who fought with the Grenadier Guards throughout the Peninsular War and at Waterloo, and Captain Augustus Charles Lennox FitzRoy of the Royal Artillery who died in 1856 in the Crimean War 'at the camp before Sebastapol, from the effect of a wound received on 8th of September while commanding in one of the advanced batteries, covering the attack on the Redan, where he had

31 Monument to Charlotte Maria, Countess of Euston (1761–1808), by John Flaxman RA, in Grafton Regis church.

greatly distinguished himself by his gallant conduct'. His cousin, the 7th Duke, who fought in the same war, was laid out for dead at the battle of Inkerman, after a bullet entered his jaw and passed out through the back of his neck, but survived and lived on until 1918, when he died at the ripe old age of 97. He was instrumental in setting up the school in Grafton Regis. Captain FitzRoy's brothers died far from home, George Henry at Nagasaki in 1868, and Arthur George in Sierra Leone in 1861.

Sir Charles Augustus FitzRoy, grandson of the 3rd Duke, played a prominent role in ruling the empire, serving as Lieutenant-Governor of Prince Edward Island, Governor-in-Chief of the Leeward Islands and Governor of New South Wales before his death in 1858. It was while he held the latter post that cedar gatherers made a settlement on the Clarence river 700 km. north of Sydney, which in about 1850 was named

Grafton in honour of FitzRoy's grandfather, the Prime Minister. The town is famed for its jacaranda festival held every year in October.

Despite the prestigious posts he held Sir Charles was not, perhaps, the role model that his masters had hoped for. As the *Centennial Magazine* acidly commented: 'FitzRoy was about as fitting a man, in every respect, as could have been picked out of the entire English nation to be sent abroad to misgovern a colony, and to corrupt its morals by his evil example. A vulgar voluptuary and systematic Sybarite, prurient, unprincipled and utterly destitute of intellectual force, he could neither govern the colony, nor his household, nor himself. He lived only for the gratification of his own base passions'.

The church was restored twice in the 19th century, in 1835–40 and 1889. On the first occasion the building was re-roofed, new pews were installed and the altar monuments were moved to a place beside the main door. Their moulded stone base was used as the reredos behind the altar. The work went on for five years at a cost of £1,100. In 1889 the floor was blocked and new choir stalls, pews, altar, rails and pulpit were erected at a cost of £400. The east window was restored and fitted with a blaze of stained glass made in Munich depicting scenes from the Parable of the Sheep and the Goats. It is dedicated to the remarkable Barwick John Sams, rector of the parish for almost fifty years, from 1837 until his death in 1885, who is reputed to have died by falling from an apple tree in the Rectory orchard. Beside the altar is a memorial to his son Charles Dawson Sams, drowned off the coast of the Pescadores on 10 October 1892, with a particularly poignant inscription from Revelations 21: 'And there was no more sea'.

The Grafton Estate

Throughout this period there were never more than four farms in the parish and about 40 cottages. The century opened with a boom in farming during the Napoleonic Wars. The Grafton estate, which owned 990 acres in the parish, benefited. Substantial increases in rent were secured after the estate was surveyed following the death of the third Duke in 1811, almost at the peak of the boom. The rent of the various tenants almost doubled: Thomas Warr's at the manor from £300 to £595 8s. p.a., William Clare's from £300 to £490 16s., John Pittam's from £250 to £512 14s., and Thomas Gallard of Paddocks Farm from £170 to £360. Joseph Smith's 46 acres of meadow and pasture was raised from £50 to £95. Even the rector was asked to pay £5 instead of £3 for his parsonage and two acres of pasture. From Lady Day 1812 the Grafton farms were yielding a total of just over £2,000 p.a. Not surprisingly, some of the tenants found themselves in difficulty within a few years of accepting these new rents. Although a report on the farms in the parish in 1819 remained optimistic, two years later Clare was slightly in arrears with his rent and Gallard rather more so. It was proposed to offer all the tenants a reduction of 10 per cent on the rents of 1812, or 12½ per cent in Gallard's case, where it was agreed that the rent was particularly high. Both he and Warr (who was talking of quitting) were to be encouraged to continue, but it was accepted that Pittam could not. Although he was not in arrears with his rent, he had neither the quality nor quantity of stock needed to run his farm successfully.

By 1830 John Pittam had duly departed and had not been replaced; likewise, Thomas Warr had given up his tenancy at the Manor where he had been succeeded by George Seabrooke. Both these farms (236 acres and 251 acres respectively) were entirely pasture, as was Joseph Smith's 52 acres of accommodation land, whereas William Clare had 52 acres of arable out of a total holding of 225 acres, and Thomas Gallard 70 acres out of 197 acres. Over the parish as a whole, only 12 per cent of the Grafton estate was under the plough in 1830.

Captain FitzRoy's arrival at the Manor in 1833 coincided with the death of Thomas Gallard the same year, although his executors kept on his tenancy of Paddocks Farm (218 acres), until at least 1844. This was the only other farmhouse in the village in these years, when the rest of the estate was let as accommodation land, the largest holding being that of Thomas and William Pell (106 acres). By 1856 another Thomas Gallard had taken over Paddocks Farm, now 173 acres, and a further 114 acres was let to Harry Linnell of Bozenham Mill Farm in Hartwell. There were eight parcels of accommodation land, all under 35 acres.

Grafton Fields

A major change in the 1840s was the building of a new farmhouse, Grafton Fields, outside the village, west of the main road, on land that had once formed part of Sties Field, where James Linnell farmed 175 acres. Grafton Fields was the only example in Grafton itself of 'model' farms which the Wakefield Lodge Estate erected in several parishes in which it was the major owner, either on the edge of a village or on enclosed common field land outside. The new farmstead, of stone with a slate roof, followed a standard design and layout similar to those built elsewhere on the estate. It was the only large new building anywhere in the parish in the 19th century, which was otherwise confined to a pair of semi-detached cottages on Church Lane and a National school (with house attached), which in 1873 replaced an old farmhouse on the main road at the northern edge of the village.

During the depressed years of the 1880s the Grafton Regis tenants shared in the general reduction of farm rents across the entire estate, first of 25 per cent in 1882–3, and then a further 10 per cent on the reduced figure in 1887–8. In 1892 John Cook Brafield's rent at Grafton Fields, where he was now farming 371 acres, was reduced from £371 p.a. to £341, enabling him to clear accumulated arrears of £170 by 1896. There was no further change in the rent until he gave up the tenancy in 1909; his successor, J.S.C. Bosworth, took the farm from Lady Day 1911 at £399 p.a. The Brafields also had Paddocks Farm and about 55 acres in these years, paying £58 p.a. until 1904 and £52 after that date. Between 100 and 150 acres in Grafton continued to be let with Bozenham Mill Farm in these years, and there were other parcels of accommodation land rented by farmers from adjoining parishes. By the 1870s Grafton Fields, now in the hands of Brafield, had grown to 215 acres, mainly through taking over land previously let to Thomas Gallard.

Grafton Park

By the beginning of the 19th century, both Grafton and Potterspury had been entirely disparked. In the early 1820s the land was divided between two large farms centred on the main houses on the estate, Grafton Lodge (270 acres, let at £380 p.a.) and Pury Lodge (470 acres, £574 p.a.), with a further 180 acres lying towards Paulerspury let as accommodation land at £180 p.a. There was one smallholder and 72 acres of woods in hand, so that the entire estate of 995 acres was let at £1,135 p.a., very close to the estimated annual value of £1,158. Most of the land on all three farms was pasture or meadow, partly because much of it was too heavy to be suitable for corn, but also because the land in Alderton, Potterspury and Grafton remained free of tithe unless it was sown with corn (the Yardley Gobion and Paulerspury portions, by contrast, were subject to heavy tithes of all kinds). Even for grass, the accommodation land at Paulerspury was 'weak, cold and poor', although it could be improved by folding with sheep. The ploughed land was heavy clay in need of much shallow draining but similarly capable of bearing good wheat and beans when folded with sheep. On the Potterspury portion of Pury Lodge farm, only two fields were ploughed for turnips and the rest kept as pasture, to avoid the imposition of tithe, but it was observed that if the tithes could be purchased much of the land would be worth ploughing, since it would be more productive in tillage than in poor greensward (grassy turf).

In 1828 the tenant of the accommodation land gave up his holding, which was divided between the two other farms, one of which also changed hands at the same time. From Michaelmas that year Grafton Lodge was let to William Bull at £560 p.a. and Pury Lodge (now 342 acres) to John Kendall at £620 p.a. In 1833 rents at both Wicken and Grafton Park were reduced by 10 per cent and John Roper, who had then recently been dismissed as the Duke of Grafton's agent and thus had to give up his farm at Potterspury, took over Grafton Lodge at £500 p.a., where he was succeeded by his son John Clarke Roper in 1838, while Kendall was paying £570 p.a. for Pury Lodge. Both rents remained unchanged until at least 1849. Besides repairs, charitable donations and other routine outgoings, the Mordaunts were spending regular sums throughout the second quarter of the 19th century on draining their Grafton Park estate. In 1883 a detached 16 acres of Alderton at Dunmore Meadow, at the northern end of the parish, was added to Grafton.

The White Hart

In the 1830s and 1840s the White Hart, named after successive monarchs' love of hunting deer in the forest surrounding Grafton Regis, was let to Robert Warr, together with 33 acres of land, for £80 p.a.; in 1856 the licensee was Stephen Blunt. In the early 1890s the pub, identified as the White Hart in estate rentals, was in the hands of Edwin Webb, who also had 29 acres of meadow in Grafton and another 40 acres near the canal at Slapton for a total rent of £69 p.a. He was succeeded by J. Stewart in 1897, followed by Henry Chapman, who remained licensee until his death in 1908. Surveys of 1875 and 1901 also list the smithy, which in the latter year was occupied by Harry Rogers. The premises were offered to the tenant at 15 years' purchase in advance of the sale of December 1920 but neither then nor at the auction was a buyer forthcoming.

The Court and Nonconformity

Surviving manor court minutes for Grafton (as for the other manors on the Wakefield Lodge estate) end in 1801 but Baker noted in the 1830s that a court was still held in the village at which the constables for Grafton and other townships were appointed. In May 1815 the constables and tenants were summoned to a court at the White Hart for the townships of Grafton, Alderton, Ashton, Hartwell, Roade, Abthorpe and other villages. A constable presumably continued to be appointed for Grafton until the Northamptonshire Constabulary stationed a man in the village, as had certainly happened by the end of the century.

In 1832 the poor rate for Grafton at 5s. in the £ raised £291 10s., although in the absence of any vestry records it is impossible to say how this income was disbursed. From 1834 Grafton became part of Potters-pury poor law union but even after the establishment in 1894 of Potterspury Rural District Council, made up of the Northamptonshire parishes of the union, such a small village rarely troubled the authority. Early in 1896 the R.D.C. considered installing a new drain at Grafton, but appear not to have proceded with the scheme. There were then said to be no complaints about the quality of the well-water on which the 150 inhabitants relied, nor with the drainage of sewage into ditches leading to the Tove. Also in 1896 there was a problem over General FitzRoy's nomination as the councillor for the parish, even though he was the only candidate, since his proposer was found not to be a resident elector.

Two houses at Grafton, those of Joseph Adkins and William Seers, were registered as meeting houses in the early 1830s. Both appear to have been short-lived ventures, since no return was made by a dissenting congregation in Grafton in the census of 1851. In the 1870s and early 1880s the Wesleyan Methodists had a 'preaching place' with 30 sittings (presumably the village school) at Grafton Regis, which had been given up by 1891. This was possibly organised by a branch of the congregation at Alderton, where a rudimentary chapel was erected in this period.

The School

A National school serving the combined parishes of Grafton Regis and Alderton was established in 1844, chiefly through the initiative of the incumbent, B.J. Sams, who also set up Sunday schools in each parish. In February that year the mistress of the Northampton Central Girls' School, which was run by the Northamptonshire branch of the National Society, provided a reference for Ann Cooper, saying that she would be 'quite able to manage the school at Grafton', having spent a week at the infants' school in Northampton, several weeks at the infants' school at Aynho and three weeks at the central school in Northampton, which served as a training centre for teachers in village schools in the county. There appears to have been no school of any sort in either Alderton or Grafton before this date. The new venture was supported by a grant of £3 12s. from the local branch of the National Society, with which the school was in union and thus under diocesan inspection.

If Ann Cooper was the first mistress at Grafton, she did not stay for very long, since a Miss West was in charge in 1847. She was followed by a succession of later teachers. The school had no premises of its own in these years and was presumably conducted from one of the cottages. When the local branch of the National Society conducted a census of provision in anticipation of the 1870 Elementary Education Act, it was found that the school occupied some 300 square feet, with a single teacher. Serving a population of about 360 in the two parishes, it had accommodation for 37 children, although there were only 11 boys and 19 girls on the books. No figure was forthcoming for average attendance, but an annual income from school pence of £3 10s. suggests the number may have been about 20. Voluntary subscriptions provided a further £15 5s. a year. Besides the day school, there were night schools in both Alderton and Grafton, the latter open two nights a week for the five winter months of the year, with 13 pupils aged between 12 and 21 and two under 12. The new Act would require the provision of 70 places at the day school, and the cost of providing an additional 33 on top of the existing 37 was estimated at £118 10s., although the parish was already said to be 'contemplating the erection of a new school'.

This was indeed what happened, as the school was reorganised to conform with the requirements of the 1870 Act. The Duke of Grafton provided a piece of land at the road junction at the northern end of the village, and in October 1871 a trust was established on standard National Society lines, with the rector, the four churchwardens for the two parishes and two other churchmen (who had to contribute at least 20s. to the school's funds) as managers. The head was to be a member of the Church of England. The school was to be under both diocesan and departmental inspection, with the bishop responsible for disputes concerning religious instruction and the bishop and Lord President jointly responsible for all other matters.

Plans were provided in January 1872 by a local architect, Edward Swinfen Harris jun. of Stony Stratford, for a stone-built schoolroom measuring 36 ft by 16 ft and 15 ft high, with a two-bedroom house for the mistress attached. There were separate playgrounds for boys and girls in front of the school and a large garden behind the mistress's house. In all the site occupied 1,080 square yards, three-quarters of which was taken up by the playgrounds. The building, which was also used for a Sunday school and parish entertainments, opened on 19 May 1873, with accommodation for 72 pupils.

A new mistress, Ada Frances Smith, was appointed in 1883. Miss Smith married a local farmer, Harry Brafield, and remained at the school, assisted only by a series of monitresses and pupil teachers, until her retirement in 1923. She was by far the longest serving mistress and had charge of the school throughout its late Victorian and Edwardian heyday, when there were 40 or more pupils on the roll. The school was also well supported in this period by both the rectors, who taught religious instruction as well as taking the chair at managers' meetings and after 1903 acting as correspondent with the local education authority, and the occupants of the manor, General FitzRoy and Colonel Lombe, both of whom served as managers. In 1899 the Duke of Grafton himself attended a managers' meeting. Apart from a dispute in the early 1890s between Mrs Brafield and the rector, in which the managers entirely supported the mistress and the bishop eventually moved the incumbent, these appear to have been happy years for the school.

Mrs Brafield's salary was raised from £59 to £65 p.a. in 1898 and by a further £5 from 1901, plus a 'donation' or bonus of £5 (including £2 superannuation), provided reports from H.M.I. and grants remained satisfactory. She also had the help of a pupil-teacher paid £18 4s. a year. Between them they taught children of all ages in a single room, divided into two by a curtain and warmed by a coal fire in the winter. The children came from both villages, those from Alderton walking over the fields, bringing their lunch with them. In general, Mrs Brafield's reports from H.M.I. were satisfactory, even if, as the years went by, her methods were seen as increasingly old-fashioned. Discipline was always highly praised and the teaching described as 'painstaking' or 'industrious', although in 1907 an inspector suggested that it might be 'more sympathetic and less mechanical'. In 1920 another hinted that in such a small school discipline need not be as rigid as was the case at Grafton, with ordinary class teaching giving way to more individual methods.

Until the First World War the school's financial position appears to have been satisfactory, although in 1898 the Education Department noted a falling off in voluntary subscriptions. On the other hand, in addition to the government grant, the school received an annual gift of £10 from the Duke of Grafton and in 1903 the parish agreed to levy a voluntary school rate of 2d., as had been done in previous years. The accounts for 1901–2 showed that a grant of £94 5s., combined with subscriptions of £24 17s. 4d., produced a slight excess of income over expenditure, of which £84 7s. out of a total of £118 16s. 4d. was represented by salaries.

The only charity traced by the commissioners in 1825 was an annual payment of £1 arising from a parcel of land allotted to the poor by the Act of 1727 confirming the enclosure agreement, which in the early 19th century was vested in the Duke of Grafton, with whose estate it appears to have been amalgamated.

GRAFTON REGIS
SINCE 1900
by Keith Harry

Introduction

In this part of the book we present a portrait of Grafton Regis at the end of the 20th century—of the changing context in which the village exists, of its buildings, of the one hundred or so people who live here, and of the remaining visible traces of Grafton's extensive history. We also look back to the beginning of the century to see the full extent of the changes which have occurred over one hundred years. Then, by drawing together the information and the memories we have gathered from present and past villagers and from others who have known the village and its people in earlier years, we will try to plot how particular aspects of village life have changed across the years.

Grafton today

The extensive growth of Northampton and the development of Milton Keynes as a new town had a significant effect on Grafton Regis during the second half of the 20th century. Their physical presence has imposed itself on the village in a number of ways. Most obviously, the lights of Milton Keynes are clearly visible from Grafton at night, and the lights and sounds of traffic on the A508, the Milton Keynes–Northampton link road, frequently disturb the tranquillity of the village. Although Grafton's predominantly rural character is still admired in 2000, it appears from photographs from the early 20th century that the nature of its rurality has been transformed over the years. Today's busy main thoroughfare, complete with street lights and speed restriction, was then a quiet, narrow country road overhung with trees. The presence of a large number of tall, mature trees, many of them elms, throughout the village is one of the most striking features of early photographs, as are the widespread grass verges. Some impressive trees remain, particularly in the grounds of the Manor and the Old Rectory, as do most of the verges, but over the years many trees have fallen victim to old age, storm and disease.

Communications

A remarkable feature of Grafton in 2000 is its close proximity to many major routes of communication. The A508, formerly the main route from London to Nottingham, has become a very busy road between the two large and expanding population centres of Milton Keynes and Northampton. The road also provides a link to the nearby M1, whose overspill travels up or down the A508 when there are delays on the motorway. The M1 had an even more direct impact on Grafton in the 1960s when the remaining cottages to the west of the A508 were pulled down. Ron Plummer recalls that the cottages had been under threat since before 1939 when a road-widening project was first proposed, which the advent of war delayed.

Maurice Allen describes the A508 before the Second World War and before it was widened:

> The main road was metalled but very narrow. There were a few heavy lorries using it. I remember one firm, W. Coe, with their solid-tyred lorries, so very noisy, especially when they picked up speed going downhill. They used to rattle and crash. They had no suspension, I do not think they even had springs.

Some of the traffic may have been noisy, but Ron Allen's pen picture of the scene outside Percy Morton's shop opposite the end of Church Lane in the 1930s indicates that there was little of it:

32 The main road to Yardley Gobion *c.* 1910.

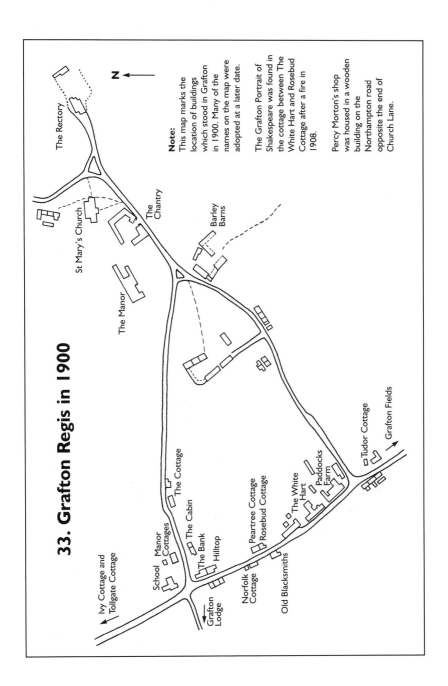

33. Grafton Regis in 1900

The Rectory

N ←

St Mary's Church

The Chantry

The Manor

Barley Barns

Note:
This map marks the location of buildings which stood in Grafton in 1900. Many of the names on the map were adopted at a later date.

The Grafton Portrait of Shakespeare was found in the cottage between The White Hart and Rosebud Cottage after a fire in 1908.

Percy Morton's shop was housed in a wooden building on the Northampton road opposite the end of Church Lane.

Ivy Cottage and Tollgate Cottage

School   Manor Cottages   The Cottage

The Bank   The Cabin

Hilltop

Grafton Lodge

Norfolk Cottage

Peartree Cottage   Rosebud Cottage

Old Blacksmiths

The White Hart

Paddocks Farm

Tudor Cottage

Grafton Fields

The AA man on his pedal cycle (with his tool pouch attached to the crossbar) and the local Police Constable from Potterspury (on his pedal cycle with his cape slung over the handlebars) could often be seen on the steps of the shop. Motor traffic was very light in those days and could usually be heard approaching from half a mile or so away.

John and Margaret Colgrove took on the tenancy of Paddocks Farm in 1956 and also recall the condition of the road:

The main road was much narrower then with just a narrow footpath barely wide enough for a pram beyond our railings at the front door, so after rain the spray from lorries and buses used to splash all over our kitchen window.

If there was a bus travelling in each direction, they could not pass on the hill outside Tudor Cottage. One would have to wait at the top of the hill until the other had gone in the opposite direction. When the road was widened in 1961, quite a lot was taken off the top of the hill, leaving it less steep than before.

Pete Plummer recalls some of the village-owned transport around this time:

I remember Mr Bull the chauffeur who lived in the Chantry, and the Reverend Cartman, who had massive whiskers that grew out of his cheekbones, and a black and yellow car. I think it was a Lanchester, but there weren't that many cars in the village. Colonel Hedley had one, I can't remember what, but I can remember Mr Holloway, the Prudential Assurance agent, buying a brand new green Morris Oxford. We had BOJ 806, a 1936 Austin Ruby, and Fred [Odell] who lived with us had NM 6261, a 1925 big-port AJS. In fact, Fred had three motorcycles more or less the same, and 'for reasons of economy you won't understand, boy' they all had the same registration number. Too young to ride pillion, I had to sit in front of Fred on a sack folded over the petrol tank. It was dangerous and I loved it. It was also illegal, but according to folklore Sergeant Ostle and Fred had an understanding.

Robin Rogers remembers Bill Allen's car and his unorthodox way of keeping it going:

Bill had a Singer car; in fact, he had a second one to supply spares for the first. The car usually had a leaking radiator, and it was necessary to put a handful of chicken meal in the radiator water about once a week.

Two of the communication routes which existed in 1900, the Grand Junction Canal and the railway, have survived virtually unchanged in physical terms. The character and function of the canal, however, have changed substantially. It is now populated for most of the year by holidaymakers travelling in relaxed fashion through the countryside on specially adapted narrow boats. There are still a few working boats, but the freight traffic of 1900 has transferred almost totally to the roads and railways. The distinct culture of the canal-dwellers of the 19th and early 20th centuries has also vanished. The main importance of the canal to Grafton in 2000 is in bringing customers to the White Hart public house, and no longer in transporting essential supplies to the people of the village. It also provides, north and south along the towpath, two of the best walks available to villagers and visitors.

There is another, very unusual, water transport link with Grafton. This is the Duke class Type 23 frigate HMS *Grafton*, which came into service with the Royal Navy in 1996, the eighth of a line of ships to be named after the dukedom dating back to 1679. HMS *Grafton* is predominantly an anti-submarine frigate, with a crew of 185 and an extensive range of sophisticated weaponry. The ship is based at Portsmouth as part of the 4th Frigate Squadron, but is affiliated to the town of Ipswich and has established strong ties with the Duke and Duchess of Grafton.

The route of the nearby main-line railway has remained unchanged throughout the 20th century, but from the perspective of the population of Grafton the railway has moved further away. This is because the nearest stations at Roade and Castlethorpe closed in the 1960s. A new station, Milton Keynes Central, has opened, but at a distance of nine miles to the south. Another original station, at Wolverton, is a few miles closer but does not have as wide a range of services as Milton Keynes.

Grafton does not have a major international airport in very close proximity—London Luton Airport, the closest, is around 30 miles away—but is frequently overflown. It is not uncommon in 2000 for four or five aircraft to be visible in the sky at the same time, on their way to or from Luton, Stansted, Heathrow, Gatwick, Birmingham, East Midlands or some more distant airport. Royal Air Force planes are also common, frequently flying so low that they send the village cats scurrying for cover. On a clear night, the sky is full of still and moving lights. Helicopters also frequently pass over, and on the weekend of one of the major events in the motor-racing calendar, the British Grand Prix at Silverstone, the sky is alive with them and loud with the sound of their engines as they transport officials and spectators from makeshift landing sites in local fields. For a number of years this event has taken place on the second weekend in July, but in 2000 the Grand Prix was held at Easter, at the end of April and was badly affected by the wet weather.

Survivals from the past: Grafton's visible history

Earlier chapters describe the historical events and the sites which are part of Grafton's history. But what remains to be seen in 2000 of such a rich past? Some of the evidence of the oldest history is now below the ground, and only appears to the untrained observer as earthworks or patterns or irregularities on the ground. David Hall and Tony Brown have described their own discoveries of Roman sites and of Roman and pre-Roman artefacts respectively. There is little to be seen of the Roman sites, but it still possible to see the covered remains of the Hermitage, excavated in 1964, to the north-west of the village; of the medieval house platforms and subsequent quarrying in the field in the middle of the triangle of village roads; of medieval fishponds on the south-east of the village on the slope down from the Old Rectory to the Grand Union Canal; of Henry VIII's Gallery, to the north of The Lane; and of ridge and furrow in the fields running down to the canal.

Joe Sargeant describes the remarkable discovery of the Hermitage:

> In the early 1960s I wanted to plough up Park Close and plant cereal crops. However, on the hill stood a pond and some rough land. The plan was to smooth the land and fill the pond in. So in came the bulldozer to start the work. Within minutes, the blade of the bulldozer struck a large stone some eighteen inches square which seemed to have a carving on it. Clearly, all progress had to stop with such a find, but I tried unsuccessfully for many months to get anybody to come and investigate. In those days, all people were interested in were Roman ruins, not medieval ones. Eventually the site was excavated in 1963 and 1964.

Much archaeological and other work remains to be done in Grafton Regis, not only to discover more about the sites already mentioned, and in particular about Henry VIII's palace, but also about some of the surviving buildings. It is hoped that this will be achieved with the help

34 The Rectory early in the 20th century.

of English Heritage and architectural historians. A remarkably high proportion of the buildings in Grafton date from the 17th century and before. These include the church of St Mary the Virgin, Grafton Lodge, the Manor (one of whose outbuildings incorporates the last surviving remnant of Henry VIII's palace), the White Hart, Paddocks Farm, Grove Cottage, Ivy Cottage and Tudor Cottage. Grove Cottage was formerly divided into three cottages known as 1–3 Thatched Cottages, but there is evidence to show that it was originally one. The building may be medieval and is believed to have architectural features which make it a rare survival. There are also a number of wells in the village, some of them of considerable age, at least one dating back to the 13th century.

It is apparent from the first part of the book that a considerable amount of research has already been undertaken, for example by David Hall on Grafton's field systems, by Glenn Foard on medieval Grafton and on the Civil War siege, by Bob Kings and the Midlands Archaeological Research Society on the progress of the siege, and by the Victoria County History on a wide range of aspects of life in the village as described in the enormous volume of estate and other records which have survived. There are also several other reports, the full text of which are on the Grafton CD-ROM, which describe the findings of individual excavations, for example on the two skeletons discovered by Sonia and Tony Baker at Grove Cottage in Church Lane, and about the finds made by Anglia Water in the course of digging by the canal. The skeletons were found during restoration work on Grove Cottage, one alongside a window and another within the walls.

Finally, there is a piece of Grafton Regis's history which is visible in Manchester, in the University's John Rylands Library. This is a painting which is known as the Grafton portrait of Shakespeare. The painting was discovered in Grafton in the early years of the 20th century and was heralded as the earliest known portrait of William Shakespeare. The portrait is no longer believed to represent Shakespeare, but the picture became so well known that the circumstances of its discovery are worth relating. In fact, a book on the topic by Thomas Kay was published in London in 1914 by S.W. Partridge & Co. Ltd entitled *The story of the "Grafton" portrait of William Shakespeare ... with an account of the sack and destruction of the Manor House of Grafton Regis by the Parliamentary forces on Christmas Eve 1643*. The principal reason why the portrait was widely believed to be Shakespeare's is because it has painted upon it the date 1588 and the number 24; Shakespeare's 24th birthday was in 1588. The letters 'W + S' are also scratched on the stretcher, but Kay dismisses this as a modern addition. As to how the picture came to be found in 20th-century Grafton, the critical event was believed to be the 1643 sacking of the remains of Henry VIII's palace, on part of the site of which the present Manor was built in 1650. Pictures and other treasures are believed to have been removed from the original building, either for safety in advance of the siege or as plunder by the soldiers laying siege to and then ransacking the wrecked building.

Kay speculates that Thomas Bunning, chaplain to Lady Crane, the occupant of the former royal palace in 1643, and Anthony Smith, a prominent Grafton resident who occupied Manor Farm, which was on the site of the school (now the village hall), secured at least some of the treasures of the house on behalf of Lady Crane. The Smith family eventually moved into a house by the main road towards the White Hart which was destroyed by fire in 1908. It was from this house that the picture was sent to Winston-on-Tees in Co. Durham, where the supposed link with Shakespeare was made; the link had not been made during the period when the picture was in Grafton. Sufficient doubt was cast upon the genuineness of the portrait for it to be discredited subsequently, but the picture and its association with Grafton became very widely known.

Plate 1 Portrait of Edward IV (English School), King of England (1461–83), champion of the White Rose, the greatest general in England and husband of Elizabeth Woodville.

Plate 2 Portrait of Elizabeth Woodville (English School). The most famous of a long line of Woodvilles to live at Grafton. Famed for her beauty, she became Queen of England (1464–83) following her marriage to Edward IV. Their daughter Elizabeth of York married Henry VII, whose Tudor rose emblem, a union of the White and the Red Rose, is the symbol of Northamptonshire.

Plate 3 Portrait of Henry VIII, by Hans Holbein the Younger. The King who loved Grafton the most. He came hunting almost every year of his reign and stayed in the palatial Manor. Henry gave the village the epithet Regis.

Plate 4 Watercolour of Grafton Regis church, 1789, by Thomas Trotter. The oldest building in the village. The exterior has remained unchanged since Norman times; the interior contains some fine monuments.

Plate 5 Watercolour of the Manor, Grafton Regis, by Thomas Trotter. The medieval house, greatly enlarged by Henry VIII, was destroyed after the siege of 1643. The present building dates from the mid 17th century and later.

Plate 6 Watercolour by Isabella Sams of the Grand Junction Canal with a horse-drawn barge and the Rectory, *c.* 1880.

Plate 7 Watercolour by Isabella Sams of the main road at the southern entrance to the village, looking north, *c.* 1880. An evocative painting of the road before the coming of the motor car.

Plate 8 Watercolour by Isabella Sams of figures skating, Grafton Regis, *c.* 1880. A charming image of late Victorian life. The pond still stands to the north of the village.

Plate 9 Watercolour by Isabella Sams of the Grafton Hunt with a distant view of the church and the Manor at Grafton Regis, *c.* 1880. The Grafton was once one of the premier packs of foxhounds in England. The hounds are in full cry after leaving Grafton Cover.

Plate 10 Stained glass east window in the parish church of St Mary the Virgin, erected as a memorial to Barwick John Sams, rector for nearly 50 years, who died in 1885. His daughter Isabella was the artist whose watercolours are published here as Plates 6–9.

Plate 11 Members of the Grafton Regis Mothers' Union at Alderton Manor in the 1950s. From left to right: Mrs Annie Eggleton, Mrs Emma ('Granny') Morton, Mrs Eunice ('Granny') Allen, Mrs Charlotte Hall and Mrs Lucy Richardson.

Plate 12 HMS *Grafton*, the latest of eight warships to be named after the dukedom, pictured off Gibraltar.

35 The 'Grafton Portrait', thought to have been the earliest portrait of Shakespeare, was found in a house next to the White Hart.

Survivals from the past: Grafton's invisible history

Bob Kings, chairman of the Midlands Archaeological Research Society, has written a fascinating account of a remarkable piece of work connected with the history of Grafton. Unfortunately, lack of space precludes the inclusion of the text here, but it can be found on the Grafton CD-ROM. The work involves searching with metal detectors to find musket balls from the Civil War siege, and then plotting the finds on a map. From the computer-generated map it is hoped that a great deal more information can be deduced about the progress of the siege than is known at present. The only previous similar large-scale application of this technique is on the site of the Battle of Little Bighorn in the United States.

Buildings and services

Only two new buildings were erected in Grafton during the 19th century, the school and a pair of cottages in Church Lane. It is remarkable, particularly in view of how extensively many nearby villages have been developed, that the number of buildings in Grafton in 2000 is very similar to the number existing in 1900. The building of eight council houses during the 1930s and several detached houses after the Second World War is balanced by the demolition of all the cottages to the west of the A508 and of the cottages at the east end of the village beyond the church. The fullest details we have been able to find on all the existing and the demolished houses in the village can be found on the Grafton CD-ROM.

In 1900, many of the houses in Grafton, as well as the farms, were owned by the Wakefield Lodge Estate. The Grafton Estate still owns farms and houses, but following the major sale of 1920 and subsequent individual sales, it owns a smaller proportion in 2000 than in 1900. The new houses built during the 20th century are either in private ownership or are rented out by South Northamptonshire Council. Several of the older houses have undergone considerable change, particularly since 1980. Manor Cottage, for example, has been divided by the Estate vertically into two residences. In addition, both 1 and 2 Old Barn Cottages, originally Estate-owned and renovated in 1980, have undergone considerable extension since.

Several major village buildings have changed their function during the century. The Manor, which began the century as one of the village farms, has since been successively a private residence, a private school, a restaurant and a private head injuries unit. Another of the farms of 1900 is now the site of a private residence, Barley Barns, in Church Lane. The village school, established in 1873 to cater for the children of both Grafton Regis and Alderton, was closed in 1934 and is now the village hall, used extensively for private hire. The Old Rectory no longer houses the church rector, but is occupied by members of the FitzRoy family.

One building, the public house, has arguably not changed its function but has changed in terms of ownership, having been owned and run by the Drake family since 1997, prior to which it had been brewery-owned

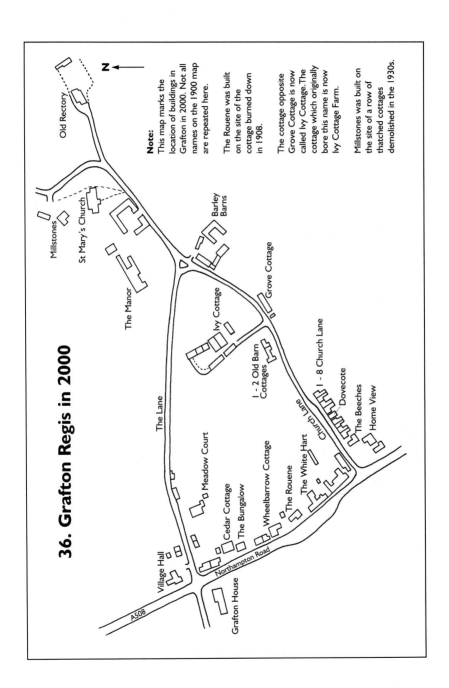

36. Grafton Regis in 2000

Note:
This map marks the location of buildings in Grafton in 2000. Not all names on the 1900 map are repeated here.

The Rouene was built on the site of the cottage burned down in 1908.

The cottage opposite Grove Cottage is now called Ivy Cottage. The cottage which originally bore this name is now Ivy Cottage Farm.

Millstones was built on the site of a row of thatched cottages demolished in the 1930s.

Old Rectory

N

Millstones

St Mary's Church

The Manor

Barley Barns

Grove Cottage

Ivy Cottage

1 - 2 Old Barn Cottages

1 - 8 Church Lane

The Lane

Meadow Court

Cedar Cottage

The Bungalow

Wheelbarrow Cottage

The Rouene

The White Hart

Church Lane

Dovecote

The Beeches

Home View

Village Hall

Northampton Road

Grafton House

A508

37 The White Hart *c.* 1911.

for many years. The character and the customers of the White Hart have certainly undergone change. Although early in the century it was claiming to cater for coach and fishing parties, in subsequent years the pub became very much the province of the working men of the village. In 2000 the White Hart's reputation for good quality food and drink attracts a wide and varied clientele not only from Grafton itself but also from Milton Keynes, Northampton and many other neighbouring towns and villages. Grafton has retained its public house through the century, but all the other trades and services which existed in 1900 have disappeared one hundred years later.

One service which Grafton appears never to have had is that of a doctor. Shirley Morris describes how this was dealt with in the 1940s and 1950s: 'if anyone needed the doctor, Mum would hang a white board on the fence [of Tudor Cottage, the Post Office, by the side of the A508] so Dr Reid would call in on his way past to see who needed him'. Ron Allen confirms that the system worked into the mid 1950s. The relative stability of the health service and of the local population is also reflected in Shirley's story of the doctor and the district nurse:

> When Joy [Wilson, Shirley's sister] gave birth to Andrea, she was attended by Dr Reid and the District Nurse, Nurse Bracken, the same team who had attended her own birth. Nurse Bracken had also attended Gilly's birth [Joy's husband] which, she claimed, made her Andrea's 'Granny' on both sides!

Most basic services reached Grafton at a relatively late date. By 1970 most of the village had septic tanks, but some houses were still dependent on privies with buckets that had to be emptied by hand. The village eventually had a sewerage system installed in 1990 at a cost of £750,000. Mains electricity reached Grafton in 1952 and piped water in 1957. Before piped water arrived, the village relied on wells. Robin Rogers has been down many of them:

> We went down most wells in the village and in Alderton. These were interesting, for often there was trouble with a leather valve if the well was pumped, like the one in the school playground, near Westons' gate. Then someone had to go down the well on a ladder, and we pulled the lead pipe and valve up for repair. Safety was assessed using a candle in a jar. A bit basic now! The candle would just be a check for oxygen present—if it went out it was dangerous. I did chemistry at school, and could never convince Uncle Bill that if there was methane down there from rotting vegetation, then there would be an explosion. All was well, the candle always stayed alight, and there were no bangs.
>
> We also cleaned out wells. The one in Chimp's garden [at Grove Cottage] had a narrow entrance which was quite cavernous beneath. At The Bank we had a well in the garden just across the A508. Water was removed by bucket and was stored in earthenware vessels outside the back door. It needed replenishing each day. We had a yoke to do this. That was fine, but in hot summers the well dried up, and we then had to go half way down Grafton Hill, a much more daunting prospect.

Larger creatures than men were also sometimes to be found in the well, as Ena and Ted Atkins recall:

> While we were at Grafton Lodge, a bullock fell down the well at the Cottage Farm near Queen's Oak. It survived because the well had a bell bottom, and was eventually rescued by the fire brigade, who put a cable through the fork of a nearby cherry tree and hauled it up. The split tree was there until a few years ago, and Joy Wilson remembers Mrs Atkins telling the tale at Sunday school.

Neither the Manor nor any of the farms was sold when most of the Wakefield Lodge estate was dispersed in 1919–20 and only a few of the cottages were disposed of. No building land became available as a result of the sales and the first new houses to be erected in the village for many years were two blocks of four built by the rural district council in the 1930s on the south side of Church Lane. The Grafton Estate sold the Manor in 1966, but retained some 650 acres of land in the parish, none of which has since been released for new building. Development has thus been confined to the replacement of a former farmstead near the junction of the two lanes running east from the main road by a large private house, some infilling of vacant plots, and refurbishment of existing property on the east side of the Northampton road. All the remaining cottages on the west side of the road were demolished in the early 1960s when the road was widened to improve access to junction 15 of the M1 motorway. During this decade a local guidebook suggested that owing to the decay of some of the older houses and the felling of many fine trees, the village had lost much of its beauty in recent years.

The growth of the village has been constrained since the 1970s by a policy of generally allowing no new building, which has also been partly dictated by the limited capacity of the sewerage system. Several proposals to develop a site on Church Lane alongside the pre-war council houses were turned down in the 1980s. Grafton Regis was designated a conservation area in 1991.

At the Manor General FitzRoy was succeeded in 1899 by Henry John Conant. By 1911, when Conant decided to leave, the full range of farm buildings in the yard to the south-east of the house had been joined by a motor garage. The new tenant was Major Ralph Henry Fenwick Lombe. Unlike Conant, the Lombes made the house their home and played a prominent part in village life until Mrs Lombe, whose husband died in 1930, left Grafton at the beginning of the Second World War.

The Manor was then taken by Lord Hillingdon, who for the previous twenty years had lived at Wakefield Lodge. Lady Hillingdon, however, preferred London society to life in the country and the house was not occupied a great deal in this period. After the war Grafton Manor was used as a school until 1960 and was then rented by the Martin family as their home. In 1966 the house and six acres of grounds were acquired by Mr and Mrs J.M. Cockeram, who restored the property as a private residence. After they left, a restaurant was established there, which failed after a few years. In 2000 the Manor is occupied by a private clinic specialising in treating victims of head injuries.

During the inter-war period the Dukes of Grafton remained the principal owners in Grafton Regis, including the Manor, Grafton Fields and Paddocks Farm. In 2000, the Grafton Estate continues to farm some 400 acres in the parish, with a further 250 acres let to a tenant at Paddocks Farm. Some of the cottages also remain in the hands of the estate, which is managed by the trustees of the Grafton Estate.

38 The Manor, seen from the rear shortly before the First World War.

Population

While the number of buildings in Grafton in 2000 is comparable to the number in 1900, the population in 2000, at just over 100, is significantly smaller than in 1900, when around 150 people lived in the village. This reflects the general trend away from large families living in one house towards the dispersal of family members into a number of different houses close by or at a distance. The development of Milton Keynes and easy access to it and to Northampton are important to Grafton in 2000 since they provide employment opportunities for most of the working population. We do not yet have access to the detailed picture provided by the 1901 census, but it seems fair to assume that not much had changed since 1891, when most of the male population of Grafton were agricultural labourers and most of the female population lacemakers. We can also assume that most of the men worked on farms in Grafton while most of the women worked at home in paying jobs in addition to looking after their families.

The work pattern has almost totally changed in 2000, with very few people working in the village itself. The electronic communications revolution of the 1990s has once again made working at home a practical option for part of the population, but in general terms there is no longer a distinct employment pattern to be observed in the village, only a widespread dispersal to jobs outside.

Daily life in Grafton

Major political events, national disasters and other occurences which affect large numbers of the population are extensively recorded in newspapers, books and other media. In 2000, as in 1900, details of everyday life tend to go unrecorded and can be quickly forgotten if they are not written up in diaries and other such accounts. We have tried to recapture a flavour of life as it was in the earlier decades of the 20th century. Our sources are the memories and impressions of past and present villagers, and people with some connection with Grafton. They have made their contribution to this book and to the village CD-ROM either through recorded discussions with members of the project team or through writing down their impressions, and in some cases we have been fortunate enough to have permission to draw on personal diaries. Unfortunately, many of the older inhabitants of the village have died during the 1990s, long before the resources to prepare this book became available, and a wealth of memory died with them.

One of the first things which has become apparent to the project team is that, particularly during the first half of the 20th century, the different strata of society represented in Grafton would have very different perspectives of daily life. In 1900, the majority of villagers belonged to the agricultural working class. On a different social level were the farmers and the occupants of the Manor and of the Rectory. Somewhere in between were the tradesmen and the publican. People from different social backgrounds would meet, but not as informally or as comfortably as in 2000. Felicity Taylor, granddaughter of Alexander Annand, a former rector of Grafton, notes that in the 1920s and 1930s 'most labouring men were referred to by their surname, e.g. Edwards, Gascoigne, etc.' and that 'Middle class people did not drink in pubs, but would have gone there to purchase stout, etc.' Jean Rogers, Grafton's last postmistress, is described by one of her daughters as being the first woman in the village to refuse to curtsey to Lady Hillingdon, who lived in the Manor immediately after the Second World War. Felicity Taylor notes another example of social conflict at a different level, this time involving Lady Hillingdon's predecessor in the Manor: 'for some unknown reason Mrs Lombe (a rather fearsome lady) refused to speak to the Annand family until the Jubilee in 1935, when she advanced grandly across the school yard at the fete and shook hands with my parents'.

Having noted the social divisions which existed in Grafton Regis as in the rest of rural England in 1900, we should not forget that certain conditions of life affected everyone in the village regardless of their background and circumstances. There was, for example, no gas or electricity, no sewerage, mains water or mains drainage. Although rail transport was available, motor cars were still in their infancy and the Grand Junction Canal was still an important commercial artery. Radio and television had not been invented, and telephone communication was in an early stage of development. Although agricultural labourers were still hired on a basis that involved their moving from farm to farm, and although some wealthy people were able to travel for pleasure, the horizons of the village were much more confined than in 2000. Children went to school in the village and often obtained work in the village. Because they lived most parts of their lives in Grafton, people were inevitably thrown together as a community much more than the inhabitants of today.

Grafton in wartime

Grafton was fortunately not in an area which suffered damage from enemy action during the Second World War, although Mrs Fountaine records in her diary:

> In the early part of the war during the Battle of Britain and when the Coventry blitzes were taking place, we experienced many anxious moments, when we heard German bombers zooming overhead and saw the huge blaze in the sky from the fires at Coventry, and we could hear the distant firing of Ack Ack guns.

From Ron Allen's account, it was clearly impossible to forget even in out-of-the-way Grafton that the war was in progress:

> We saw a great deal of troop movement on the ground and a great deal of aircraft activity, particularly the heavy bombers forming up for raids over Germany. We later saw many aircraft towing gliders prior to the attack on Arnhem. When Coventry was bombed heavily we heard German aircraft overhead (their engines had a distinctive note) and we could see an ominous red glow in the sky. We regularly saw R.A.F. Queen Mary type long vehicles parked outside the White Hart with the remains of crashed British and German aircraft aboard. We also had laden tank transporters through the village quite frequently and many of the drivers took delight in putting their vehicles out of gear and coasting down the hills on either side at great speed. This was a highly dangerous

practice but, to their credit, they never crashed.

We often had small units of soldiers and large army vehicles occupying the Barley Barns, with large Army tanks on the green during exercises. Also, since the village stands on a hill it was very suitable terrain on which to locate mobile searchlight units with their attendant ack-ack guns, and I have seen them just inside the gate in Park Close with the crews billeted across the road in the school building. They usually stayed for a couple of weeks before changing their location.

There was a practice bombing range alongside the River Tove opposite the Tollgate and just below Alderton and this was used on a daily basis by Wellington bomber crews in training. It was a common sight to see a Wellington with an accompanying Spitfire in the skies above the village during the hours of daylight. On at least two occasions during the war, military aircraft force-landed in the field one over from the front of the White Hart. The first was a Fairey Battle, which I believe was piloted by a member of the Fleet Air Arm, and I remember going with the ground crew who came to his aid to show them how they could get their vehicle right up to the aircraft. Repairs could not be immediately effected and the Home Guard stood guard on the aircraft all night. On another occasion, a Tiger Moth put down and was there for several hours, and I recall a Spitfire putting down to bring an engine part for it.

Towards the end of the war, the young Ron and Ken Plummer came face to face with a very vivid example of the consequences of the conflict:

I wonder how many Grafton folk remember the evening of the 20th March 1944, the night the Wellington bomber crashed into the farmyard at Yardley Gobion? Ken and I were in bed when we heard the sound of an aircraft approaching—flying very low. The sound was strange, rather like a car engine when it's running out of petrol. We jumped out of bed and looked out of the window in time to see a twin-engined plane coming from the direction of Northampton—just above the trees and sort of following the A508 it seemed. We could see the plane quite clearly as one engine and part of the wing was all in flames which illuminated most of its body.

As it drew level with our window, it was more or less above Molly Holding's cottage (Sam's and Margery's at that time I think), and if TV aerials had existed in those days it would have hit it, it was that low. Anyway, it rumbled on past in the direction of Yardley and just moments later there was a loud explosion like a bomb going off—we heard the next day that it crashed in the farmyard—blowing up and killing all five crew. Ken and I saw the farmyard a few days afterwards—it had a massive crater in it and most of the farm buildings were flattened. It's sad to think that the crew were only on a training exercise at the time.

The effects of war were also felt in a number of other ways. In common with every town and village across Britain, Grafton men went to fight in the forces. Troops were billeted in the village, and the Home Guard trained there. Dick Green recalls that during the early years of the war, church services were held on Sunday afternoons because of blackout regulations. Thanks to its rural location, Grafton also received a number of evacuee children, and a number of prisoners of war were sent there to work on the land. Mrs Ward of Piddington recalls that Tom Elliott, the farm manager at Grafton Lodge and the man who employed the Irish labourers whose ghostly experience begins this book, was not impressed by the Italian and German POWs' attitude to work, but Ron Plummer recalls of the Italians that they were a very cheerful bunch, and that in their spare time they made wooden toys which they sold locally for just a little money. He recalls no animosity towards them from the villagers.

Joan Harris, who was born in Grafton in 1934 and left the village in 1949/50, recalls her experience:

My Dad [Harry Harris] was called up for the armed services. He was a soldier in the Tank Regiment and was away for long periods, but I remember him coming home on leave and I used to wait up for him. It was usually late when he arrived because public transport was very poor. We would have a cup of tea and because there was no sugar we would find a sweet and have that instead. Another time we waited in the school yard all day, meeting every bus until he finally arrived with his big kit bag. We were so happy to have him home for a few days.

During the war all road signs were taken down and we children were told never to tell anyone the name of the village. We loved it when the convoys of American soldiers came through, and would shout 'Got any gum, chum?' and they would throw packets to us from the trucks. [Robin Rogers notes that the Harris girls were much more successful at this than he was!]

In the school yard periodically soldiers were billeted using the school itself for sleeping. We loved it because they would give us food from their billy cans ... and they would let us talk on their radios.

I remember seeing searchlights in Park Close (the field opposite The Lane). Mr Bull (George, Irene Holman's dad) and Mr Garrett were ARP wardens and used to patrol the village in the evening making sure there were no lights showing from windows, etc., during the blackout. The windows were taped up in a criss-cross fashion in case of breaking glass. Torches had red paper over the glass so as not to give too much light.

We did not have an air-raid shelter but knew we had to get under the table in the kitchen if ever there was a raid when we were indoors. Gas masks were issued and we had to take them to school every day where sometimes we had gas mask practice. At first, John had a large dome contraption as he was just a baby, but later this was exchanged for a Mickey Mouse type of gas mask especially issued for toddlers.

Our clothing coupons we used to exchange for second-hand clothes. Mum had this arrangement, I think it was with some London friends of Mrs Annand. Mrs Annand would give them our clothing coupons and they would send us clothes—large parcels of dresses, suits and coats, etc.

Don Allen and John Harris also recall the soldiers, and the Home Guard on duty:

Soldiers were billeted in the old school, which had closed a few years before the War. They used to light fires in the school yard so that they could cook in the billy cans. And we often saw them practising manoeuvres in the street.

The Home Guard used to meet in the school on Sunday morning and practise down at the old brickyard. Don remembers going to watch one day and being invited by Alf Holloway to fire a live round from a .303 rifle. Don would have been no more than eight years old, and live ammunition was very scarce.

Ron Allen was a youthful member of the Home Guard:

At first they were rather a ragtag bunch, mainly consisting of those too old to be conscripted and those in reserve occupations, and were led by those with previous military experience, usually from

39 Grafton and Alderton Home Guard in the Second World War. Standing left to right: Emmanuel Hall, Bob Holloway, Will Webb, Fred Webb, Stan Markham, Sid Hall, Frank Hall. Seated: Alf Holloway, Ted Webb, Mr Eggleton, Percy Morton, William Allen.

the First World War. At Grafton, the platoon was supplemented by several men from Alderton and they were commanded by Second Lieutenant Alfred Holloway, the local Pearl Assurance agent. They made their headquarters in the old village school building, now the village hall. The Home Guard were quite well organised and reasonably well armed, although I dread to think how effective they would have been had the invasion which we all expected actually taken place.

When I was just over ten years of age, being a big lad, I lied about my age and managed to join the Army Cadet Force at Yardley along with Ron Plummer, who also lived in Grafton. We were given uniforms and told to parade with the Home Guard at Grafton, which we did regularly on Sunday mornings. Parents of today would never tolerate the kind of activities which we undertook with the Home Guard (I doubt if I ever told my own mother!). As a boy of less than twelve years old I was able to strip, assemble, load and fire a sten gun. I fired .22 and .303 rifles and a Lewis machine gun. I fired a dummy hand grenade from a cup discharger on a .303 rifle and I put detonators into hand grenades. I remember an exercise with the other Home Guard units when we were being fired upon—I did not realise at the time that they were using blank ammunition and I found it very scary. The circumstances of the day made us very mature indeed.

The Home Guard paraded every Sunday morning at 10.00 and would be taught the rudiments of handling their most recent weaponry, or go target shooting in the old quarry beyond Ivy Cottage Farm near the old Alderton turn, or alternatively take part in mock exercises in Home Hill behind the Church. The parades always finished to coincide with the lunchtime opening of the White Hart and it was not uncommon to see rifles hanging on cycles outside since the landlady objected to having them on the premises.

Felicity Taylor's experience, as a member of a family resident in Bath but with a home in Grafton, was rather different:

Before the war all the villages of England had a round yellow AA sign with the name of the village, so you always knew where you were. They were of course taken down at the beginning of the war in case the Germans, who we were expecting any day to invade us, knew where they were. Such a pity they were never replaced.

In Sept. 1939 we were at The Cottage at the outbreak of war, so we hastily dug up the veg. and picked the apples and Mother made blackberry and apple and damson jam and we fled back to Bath as we didn't know then how easy it would be to travel and what was going to happen. My brother made two trips to and fro with Mother and me and then Father and May, our maid (who left quite soon to do war work, I think in the Forces—our last live-in maid!). Both times his little Hillman Minx was loaded to the gunwales with sacks of potatoes, carrots and apples and altogether 25lb. of jam.

Of course mother could remember the food shortages in the last War only 20 years before, not long although to us it was a long time ago. In fact, my parents were able to go back there as usual in April and August/September, with help from the village (Mrs Dormer) to scrub the tile floors downstairs and so on. Mother tried to remember how to cook from her youth and struggled with the Beatrice stove and the fires, she was in her 50s then, large and rheumatic from years of damp houses, but she managed. My brother came on leave from the Army and I from the Admiralty which had come to Bath, but I only had 10 days a year off so I had 5 in April and 5 in August. Once going to bed I put my candle too close to the window, which of course had a blackout curtain. But I heard a stentorian voice from the quiet lane below 'Put that light out!' It was the air-raid warden doing his rounds, and I hastily blew out the candle.

Shops and post offices

In 2000 Grafton has no shops and no post office. The last shop in the village was the craft shop run by Sue and Peter Blake at Millstones, beyond the Church, which closed in the early 1990s. The building is now used as a holiday cottage. The village has been served for many years by a mobile fruit and vegetable van run by Cliff Brown from Yardley Gobion, and a variety of other local services are offered from outside the village, as well as a free weekly bus to the Tesco supermarket at Mereway, Northampton. The post office at The Bank closed in the early 1980s, having been located in several different places during the century; the nearest post office is now at Yardley Gobion. The White Hart, which became a public house in the mid 18th century, was bought by the Drake family in 1997, having been run by a succession of different landlords following the retirement of Arch Bushell in 1980.

The name of Percy Morton is synonymous with the Grafton shop. Having been severely wounded in the leg during the First World War, he is believed to have set up the shop with the assistance of the British Legion. Maurice Allen recalls the origins of the shop:

> Percy Morton used to have his shop further down the hill at one time next to The Slipe but had it moved to the spot opposite Church Lane at the other end of the row of cottages after it was burgled. There was not a shop before Percy had his built. I do not know how we got groceries or how we lived even, but we always seemed to have enough food in the house. My Mother could make a meal out of anything. We never had any money in the family but we always had food.

Don Allen and John Harris remember the shop in wartime:

> Most food was rationed—BU coupons for bread and B2 for sweets. Sweet rations were carefully selected at the shop, run by Percy Morton, a casualty of the First World War. The shop, a wooden building, stood at the top of a slope on the west side of the main road opposite Church Lane. On one occasion, Brenda Harris used her coupons to buy a tin of evaporated milk, which would have been all right had she not hidden it behind a plant pot on the spinet

40 Percy Morton's shop in the 1930s, with Percy, daughter Doreen, Mrs Mary Morton and Alfred ('Chimp') Richardson.

(a type of harpsichord), where it was subsequently spilled, making quite a mess!

Percy Morton's shop sold groceries and sweets, but according to Felicity Taylor it was also a place for villagers to meet:

> When we weren't working, and perhaps it was a wet morning we would walk round the village to Percy and stay gossiping in his hut, and buy a few things and sweets, and call in on his mother perhaps (Mrs Jim) or Mary Holloway.

Joy Wilson recounts what happened when Percy Morton gave up the shop:

> Molly Holding took over the shop when Percy Morton retired, and ran it from the middle room of Pear Tree Cottage, which could have measured barely twelve feet square, until late 1966. When Gil and I married in August of that year, Molly took my first grocery order, but by that time had so little stock that she was only able to supply about half of what I needed.

Percy's shop did not provide for all the needs of the village. As in 2000, some people took the bus to Stony Stratford or Northampton to shop. Other services were also available in the village in addition to the shop. Felicity Taylor lists the produce and products which she recalls being sold in or delivered to Grafton before the Second World War:

> Bread (and seed cake once a week) was good when new but got very dry, and was delivered probably three times a week from Yardley. Meat came from Yardley too, from Odell's (North and South, East and West, Odell's sausages are the best!). Milk from Brafield's (later Marchant's) farm in the village [Paddocks Farm], was delivered daily by hand-pushed churn with a dipper measure hooked on the side. One could fetch some more after the afternoon milking from the dairy. Butter was fetched from Martin's farm [Grafton Lodge] from Mr Elliott, the farm manager. Half-pounds were cut off the big slab and patted into oblongs with wooden paddles. Eggs were bought from Mr Frost, who lived on the main road in Norfolk Cottage, next to the village well (which had a bucket attached to a chain on a roller which was wound down by a handle). Mr Frost was a carrier too at one time who would get things for you. Victoria plums could be bought in August from the brick kiln cottage at the bottom of the hill on the left going to Northampton, and honey from the Masons at the post office. Pork pies, potted meat, fruit, vegetables and fish, were obtained from a

weekly trip to Northampton on market day. Mother also changed her book at Boots subscription library. Newspapers were delivered daily from Percy Morton's shop and the post was delivered sometimes twice a day. The public telephone was near the White Hart [as it is in 2000], and telegrams could be sent from the post office.

Maurice Allen also recalls the deliveries which used to come to Grafton, including his own paper round:

> I used to deliver the *Football Echo*, a green paper always known as 'the Green 'un'—twelve in all round the village and I was paid three pence for that. The Holloways always asked me in whilst they found the money to pay for their paper, so I got to know the inside of their house. I think it was only a penny in those days, but they used to let it run on for two or three weeks.
>
> The butcher used to come round twice a week, Odell from Yardley. He was known as Tebby. The wage in those days was thirty bob [£1.50], so not much to spend on meat. The baker, also from Yardley, was Mr Beryl, a lovely old boy who came two or three times a week. He had a proper two-wheel baker's cart on which he would go along singing 'The more we are together the merrier we shall be'. His bakery was just past the pond behind Shakeshafts' shop in Yardley. We often used to go in there on the way home from school just to get warm.

The last Grafton postmistress was Jean Rogers, who ran the post office at The Bank on the Northampton road. At the beginning of the century, the post office was located in Church Lane at what is now 2 Old Barn Cottages, and subsequently it was relocated to The Cabin in The Lane, and then to Tudor Cottage on the Northampton road. The volume of work in the post office must have been very limited, but rules were rules, as a young Chimp Richardson found to his cost. Charles Reece relates the story:

> One day, Chimp's mother sent him to Grafton [from Bozenham] to buy a stamp and post a letter. It was a cold winter's day with a bitter east wind, and to make matters worse, Chimp was only wearing short trousers. He arrived at the post office [in The Cabin] just before Mrs Wilcox was about to close for lunch. As he approached, he saw Mrs Wilcox peer through the window and proceed to lock the door, knowing full well that Chimp was

outside. Left with no choice, Chimp had to wait the full hour
outside, desperately trying to keep warm. One hour later, he bought
the 2d. stamp, posted the letter, and walked into the east wind all
the way back to Bozenham, one very cold boy!

Fortunately, the post office did not always have such a bad public image,
as Joy Wilson records:

> From 1948 to 1965, the post was delivered each morning by Irene
> Holman. The postman would deliver it to the post office, which
> was in the corner of the living room at Tudor Cottage. Mother
> sorted it into village order then Rene packed it into a bag or into
> her bicycle basket and set off on what was supposed to be a
> walked post round but, bearing in mind it included Grafton Lodge,
> Grafton Fields Farm and The Tollgate, was over six miles. On the
> odd occasion that someone came from head office to check the
> round, I remember Rene used to be pretty tired by the time she
> finished! Every dog in the village knew the post lady as Rene
> never did her round without a pocketful of biscuits and she would
> even stop to feed crumbs to a robin which met her in The Lane.
>
> It was not only the wildlife which received sustenance from
> Rene. In conversation with Hylda Reece, Ena and Ted Atkins
> recalled that in the course of her round Rene also delivered 60
> cigarettes a day to Hylda at Grafton Lodge, leaving them under a
> bucket. Hylda's husband Ted, himself a pipe smoker, thought
> Hylda had packed up!

Natural history in Grafton

In the early years of the century, some components of the natural history
of the village were more important as sources of food than as sources of
admiration, as Maurice Allen describes:

> There were no big-time poachers about then, but I think everyone
> would poach for a Sunday lunch. I never remember seeing a
> pheasant served even if we took one home—it would always be
> chicken by the time it reached the table! My oldest brother Bill
> was a great fisherman. He knew exactly where to drop his line and
> what he was fishing for, and he always got it. He always brought
> them home, maybe roach or perch which other people would throw
> back, but Mother always cooked them because we expected them

to be cooked. Sometimes it would be a pike—it was a big thing if you got something like that. There were a lot of eels in the River Tove.

There was also a close link between Robin Rogers's family and the natural history of the village in the 1950s, which must have been shared by many villagers:

> It seemed that we mainly lived on rabbit pie. Rabbiting was as much a part of normal life as wooding. Most nights we would catch a rabbit or two. We always had a stick over the shoulder, about three feet long, one inch in diameter with a knob on the end. If you saw a rabbit hiding in a tuft of grass the sequence was to wallop the animal as hard as you could, and then finish it off by wringing its neck.
>
> All this seems very callous now, but then in the fifties, it was part of the culture. I cannot remember being hungry, but without those rabbits, the odd pigeon and pheasant, it would have been a lean existence. Mother said that they used to catch the sparrows when she was a girl, and eat the breasts. Fortunately we didn't get a chance, but when we visited Aunt Phyll at Castlethorpe, rook pie was not so rare. This was a grey meat, and was definitely an acquired taste.
>
> We had eggs from the hens across the road, and in the season we used to get moorhen eggs to fry. You had a long hazel pole on to the end of which was tied a spoon. You could get eggs then without risking falling in a pond. We used to get eggs from the pond at the bottom of Weston's field, opposite Colonel Hedley's, from the Flats pond, and from the ponds in Park Close, as well as a few others.

But Maurice Allen also expresses an appreciation of the beauty of the countryside around the village in the late 1920s and early 1930s:

> One of the fields with Grafton Lodge Farm was The Ground, a forty-acre field one over from Park Close. It was the only place I knew where harebells grew and they grew in profusion. The whole field was a cloud of blue, then later in the year it was almost as blue with small blue butterflies, masses of them; I do not recall seeing them anywhere else.

Gilbert and Joy Wilson (Maurice Allen's niece) have had a lifelong interest in the natural history of the village and have some vivid memories:

> We remember sitting in the Great Meadow with our two children in the early seventies in a corner which did not lend itself to mowing. We sat apart after our picnic and had a contest to see who could pick the greatest number of different grasses in a given area. We were told by a passer-by to enjoy the moment as the land was scheduled for ploughing. Sure enough, once the hay was mown the drainage people moved in and that autumn land which had been meadow for generations fell under the plough to provide yet more acres for rape.
>
> We also recall standing at the field gate opposite The Cottage, from where Gilbert saw a bird fly into the cover, in spring 1977. Was it a cuckoo, or was it a sparrowhawk? We spent an entire afternoon crawling through blackthorn bushes and trees, several of which he climbed only to find old crows' nests, until at last he found a nest containing five sparrowhawk's eggs. It was one of only two recorded nesting sites in Northamptonshire that year. Now, twenty three years on, the species has reached almost pest proportions.
>
> In 1971 there was a heron's nest in the oak tree along the hedge from the barns over the canal bridge. It was joined by a second nest in the following year. Unfortunately, they were disturbed by egg collectors, since when we have had no herons nesting in the parish. During the eighties, short-eared owls visited the rough ground near the paper mill each winter, but they have not been seen for several years. Long-eared owls often over-wintered in the Cover. During the shooting season, guns had to be warned of their presence so that none would be harmed accidentally. Red kites, released by conservationists a few years ago, can be seen by the keen observer, and have now been joined by buzzards, which had not been seen in the vicinity for a number of years until recently.
>
> For over twenty years, until the late nineties, curlews nested in the fields to the south of the village. As many as half-a-dozen could be seen at the same time. For some years through the eighties, a flock of as many as two hundred golden plovers visited the meadows bordering the River Tove in mid-April, but would stay only a few days. When the river is in spring flood, even now we are visited by numbers of widgeon and pintail. Later, house martins and swallows seem to follow the waterways as they return from their winter migration. Whinchat, stonechat, redstart and

wheatears all seem to follow this route during spring.

In the early spring of 1992, Mont Castle rang from Old Barn Cottages to say that 'something' had killed his hens, taking one away and leaving the others dead in the pen. A trap set that night caught the culprit, a mink, the first recorded in the village. Since then, regular trapping on the banks of the Grand Union Canal and in hedgerows leading away from the canal has caught at least one hundred more. As a result, the coot, moorhens, ducks and water voles, which had almost disappeared, have made a welcome return. Rabbits, decimated by myxamatosis in the fifties, had by the nineties almost recovered to their former numbers.

The village lost as many as three hundred mature elm trees to Dutch elm disease during the 1970s, and now at the new Millennium our ash trees seem to be suffering from disease. First a few odd branches went, but very soon after several quite mature trees have died. We still have a stand of eight to ten mature elm trees in the parish at the end of Ruggs Lane, about half a mile west of Grafton Fields Farm. As far as we know there are no others in the county.

I recall the end of the fine horse chestnut tree which stood in the field behind Old Barn Cottages and near the yard of Paddocks Farm:

> The tree was a landmark. Travelling towards Grafton along the A508 past the Yardley turn, you could see it looming above Old Barn Cottages. It was a wonderful sight in flower and leaf and was full of birds, being a nesting site for many jackdaws, which now nest in any uncovered chimney in the village. The foliage had been looking a little thinner than usual for a couple of years prior to its being blown down. It survived the first, great storm of 16 October 1989, but fell late one afternoon in another storm several months later in January 1990 with its enormous root system facing back towards the cottages. This was so huge that it dwarfed the horses which frequently sheltered under it. It took years for the whole of the tree to be cut up and removed.

Much natural beauty remains in Grafton and its locality. One special site is Mill Crook Hay Meadow Nature Reserve, a traditionally managed 14-acre hay meadow situated close to Grafton in the valley of the river Tove. It was purchased from Jack Weston of Yardley Gobion by the Northamptonshire Wildlife Trust in 1989 as it was feared that a change of ownership was about to occur and that damage could be sustained under a less sympathetic owner. The type of grassland which the meadow represents is very rare, nationally as well as locally. It contains over 20 different grass species and a wide range of other plants. As well as being a good place to see a kingfisher, the reserve is alive with insect life in the summer months.

Farming and other trades in Grafton

Grafton was very much an agricultural community before the Second World War. Maurice Allen provides an insight into the work of his father William Allen, both on the farms of the locality and at home, and into the day-to-day pressures which affected farm workers and their families:

> My father used to like a drink, rather too much I'm afraid, until I consider how he worked. He used to be away at work all week, and it was hard work, and then at weekends he used to come home to gardening, digging spuds or planting cabbages and mending all our shoes and so on. We did not have new shoes very often and not realising how short money was we children used to kick the toes out of them, sometimes deliberately kicking them against the wall. I realise now that I have raised a family of my own how hard it must have been although I did not have to work anything like as hard as he did.
>
> His job was driving an agricultural steam engine. When they finally finished with these engines they were brought back and parked in the Barley Barns where they stayed for years. There is a photograph somewhere of Mother and Father sitting on the front of the engine. They would have one engine either end of the field with a wire rope between to plough. It would take about two days to plough a field like this, now it would take a couple of hours. They would go round several farms and work long hours to get a living. When he came home, often cycling twenty miles or more, he would stop at the pub for a couple of drinks and maybe one more than he should have, so there was often a row between he and Mother when he returned. He would still go off to do his gardening in the afternoon and often stop for another drink on his way back which would start another row. He would still do whatever jobs needed doing in the evening, often working out in the barn by torchlight. I do not know how he managed. I think I would have been permanently drunk had I been him. There always

41 William and Eunice ('Granny') Allen with the steam engine which he operated for many years.

seemed to be a certain amount of tension when he was around. As a child I always thought he was the cause of it all but looking back I think he was entitled to his relaxation before leaving at four o'clock on Monday morning to cycle back to work.

Mrs Ward of Piddington recalls the labour force at Grafton Lodge before the Second World War:

> George Atkins, Chimp, Emmanuel (Man) Hall, many of the Allens,
> Frank and Joey Lucas, all worked for Tom Elliott on the farm.
> Mabel Elliott (Tom's daughter) said you could set your clock by
> the time when the Lucas boys arrived for work from Alderton. Joe
> Sargeant, when told this story recently, added that one of them was
> always a little later than the other because he would stop to relieve
> himself at the last minute before entering the farm.

Allin Hawkshaw is a Canadian who visited Grafton briefly during the
Second World War and wrote to his parents on 24 August 1942
describing his visit:

> I spent 3 days stooking grain for a nearby farmer (Grafton Lodge).
> Labour is very scarce and many village people came out to help.
> One lady was 74 years of age; the others were younger and some
> mid-aged. I was the only male excepting the farmer (Tom Elliott?)
> who drove the harvester. Working with heavy sheaves in the hot
> sun is certainly hard work for a woman. She certainly knew how
> to put sheaves together. I was the only one that stooked by
> pitchfork. The others all picked the sheaves up by hand. They
> thought that was strange. One day the elderly lady and I said we
> would beat the other four women from one corner of the field to

42 The Hall family: Emmanuel ('Man') Hall, daughter Kathleen, son Francis ('Frank') and
wife Charlotte.

43 Grafton Lodge between the two World Wars, when J.J. Martin lived there.

the other and we did! I stooked a lot of wheat to make sure she won. She thought it was wonderful. As the wheat was being cut rabbits kept to the centre of the field before it was cut. Near the end they ran out and the elderly lady and I caught one (killed). She wanted me to take it home to Mrs Annand for dinner. I did and Mrs Annand was delighted. We had good rabbit for two dinners.

The agricultural seasons had a direct impact on most of the people in the village, not just the farmers and the farm workers, as Don Allen and John Harris recall:

We used to be given time off school at harvest time to go potato picking. We were paid for this, one shilling and three pence an hour [about 6p]. Sometimes we helped to 'shock' the corn, and when a field of corn was almost cut all the men and boys stood round with sticks waiting to kill any rabbits or rats that might run out. I remember catching live mice and then chasing Nancy Holloway with them. Nancy used to work at Paddocks Farm when Freddie Marchant was there.

Robin Rogers also took on farm work as a young man, in the fifties:

As a teenager I also did summer work on the farm. The field opposite the White Hart had one of the earliest crops of flax, and horse and cart was still the main mode of transporting the cut crop. I also spent much time baling. My job was on the sled behind the baler, stacking the bales on the sled, then releasing them off the back, steadying the swaying stack, and running to catch up the tractor and baler in time to catch the next bale to make into the next stack. The worst job was baling beans, with masses of black dust all over you. I still wonder what that did to my lungs.

When Freddie Marchant died, John and Margaret Colgrove took over Paddocks Farm:

That first summer I bought about forty beasts, then I bought four cows, and I used to buy week-old calves to multiple suckle. We could not milk because the old cowshed which we have now turned into stables would never have passed inspection for TT and we could not have afforded to build a replacement so we used to rear about forty Hereford/cross calves each year. We would put four calves to a cow to start with and after three months we would wean those and put three on them, then after two or three months another two.

We did not have a bull as it was not worth keeping a bull for four cows, so we used to have the 'AI man' come to inseminate them, usually from a Hereford bull. We did this for several years. The first milk, or bisnings, Chimp always used to take home. When we had lambs there were several ladies in the village who would cook the lambs' tails. In those days we did not cut the tails until the lambs were about three weeks old, by which time they had a bit of meat on them. Mrs Mary Holloway and Granny Allen used to cook them. We never did them ourselves, but apparently they used to put them in almost boiling water and then the wool would peel off easily and then they were breadcrumbed and fried.

We used to have to take our sheep to Alderton to dip them, driving them up the main road, until we had our own sheep dip built. Bill Allen built it with reinforced concrete and following Ministry specifications, but unfortunately the Ministry dimensions had made no allowance for the fact that a sheep before shearing is wider, and so the sides of the dip had to be broken out and rebuilt.

We used to castrate the beasts by using a knife to cut them then pull down the stones and pull them out. With lambs I used to bite them out. Chimp used to help and hold them, but he could not do it because he had false teeth

During the winter of 1963, when we were snowed in for several weeks, we went across the fields to Paulerspury to fetch bread for the village. Just before the big freeze-up, British Waterways had been dredging the canal. They tipped it all into our meadow. They had taken out all the hedge along the towpath and had put up fencing either end of where they were working but there was no fence along the towpath. We had some cattle in the meadow and with the canal frozen to a depth of a foot or more the cattle just wandered across the canal into The Old Park which at that time was rented by Charlie Weston. When we got them back there was one missing. I asked Jack Weston but he said he had not seen it. It was a couple of weeks later that he rang to say that the beast had been found—hanging up in Joe Sargeant's slaughterhouse. Joe had asked Charlie Weston how long he had been keeping Irish heifers, to which Charlie replied that he did not buy them because he did not like them. Joe then told him that he had sent one for slaughter.

Women's life in Grafton

Before running water and mains electricity arrived in Grafton, such tasks as washing clothes and cooking were much more difficult and time-consuming, and it was generally women's time which was taken up in coping with these tasks. Don Allen and John Harris describe some of the conditions in which women lived their working lives, and some of the jobs which they had to do:

> A black range stood in most kitchens as a means of cooking, and some were lucky enough to have a primus stove which not only heated water much more quickly but, particularly in summer, meant that the house did not get quite so hot when cooking.
>
> On Sunday morning my Dad used to cook the small potatoes up in the copper for 'pig potatoes' to last the week. When he had finished Mum used to have to clean the copper out ready to boil her washing on Monday. (John Harris)
>
> We also kept pigs, usually two, in a garden across the road from The Bank, nearly opposite Molly's. These were fed on boiled potatoes, apples and any scraps. They were slaughtered by the butchers from Yardley (Odells). They were burned in straw to remove the hair, and bled from the throat by hannging upside down in the barn. Mum and Gran cured the meat by salting in zinc trays.

The meat was then hung in the kitchen in white cotton to protect from flies, and meat was cut from it for the rest of the year; delicious, absolutely delicious. It was a welcome change from rabbit pie. (Robin Rogers)

Granny Allen, with whom we lived, had an arrangement with the Cartmans at the Rectory. We had days picking fruit: plums, pears and apples galore. My favourites were russets. The fruit was sold from the front door of The Bank. It was weighed on a spring balance, and there was nearly world war three when a Weights and Measures inspector had the audacity to do a check on Granny's scale! (Robin Rogers)

Washday Monday was quite a busy occasion. The water for washing at Tudor Cottage had to be collected from the pump at the Council Houses reached by means of a gap in the hedge, where the ground was often quite slippery. One day when I was due to go to school to sit exams I fetched a bucket of water, sat down in the gap in the hedge, and tipped the water all over myself, pretending that I had slipped and spilled the water accidentally. By the time I was dry it was too late for school! (Don Allen)

Following a long tradition, women also performed a number of functions which are now undertaken by professionals, for example, laying out the dead. Maurice Allen's mother undertook this task in Grafton:

My mother would help anybody. If anyone died they had to be laid out in a special way and I think they put pennies over their eyes or something. It was Mother they usually called upon, and I remember overhearing her telling Father that when she was called to Mrs Frost [of Norfolk Cottage] she had to put paper over her hands to lift her up and as she did so all the skin just fell away in the paper. She had apparently been left for days before her husband called anyone.

She also had a special way of coping with the demands of the war on her family:

When the war began and Mother saw all her five sons go off into the various armed forces, her youngest daughter into the Land Army and her other three daughters already away from home, she made us all a promise. She told us whenever possible to listen to the nine o'clock news from the BBC each evening, and as we heard Big Ben strike she would think of each of her children in turn, starting with Bill who was the eldest. We would know that wherever we were in the world at the appropriate stroke, her thoughts would be with one particular child. It was a comforting thought during those dark days.

The Mothers' Union provided a social focus for women from Grafton and Alderton away from day-to-day family life. The Union was very active in the parish during the 1940s and 1950s.

Growing up in Grafton

Joan Harris recalls life when she was a child:

> I was born in 1934 and lived in Grafton until 1949/50 when I left to live in Birmingham. I was the eldest of the three children of Henry and Florence Harris (Harry and Flo). My sister Brenda was two years younger and brother John five years younger. Our home for all of my childhood was the School House behind the school (now the Village Hall) at the top of The Lane.
>
> The house consisted of the 'front room' as we always called it, which overlooked the fields, the kitchen with black range for cooking and heating, and the scullery, a lean-to building with brown stone sink. There were two bedrooms, one for my parents and one for us children with girls in a double bed and John in a single bed alongside. There was no bathroom. All our water came from the pump in the schoolyard. We had paraffin lamps (years later we had a Tilley lamp, still burning paraffin but with a mantle, which gave better light). The privy was at the bottom of the garden.
>
> The kitchen was the hub of the house as the only place that had heating. We had this large, scrubbed-top table that was used for everything from preparing food, eating, homework, playing cards, making jigsaws, etc. It was rarely cleared, just everything moved around.
>
> The front room was only used for special occasions, Christmas and some winter evenings if we had coal for the fire. Food was very basic as most of my memories are from 1939 onwards when food was rationed. We had lots of potatoes, fruit from the garden, rabbits—though I never remember feeling hungry. We ate things like bread and dripping and bread and sugar.

44 Sunday School children 1948–9: a photograph taken by Mrs 'At'. Standing left to right: John Harris, Joan Harris, Daphne 'Pinky' Weston, Doreen Morton, Shirley Allen, Brenda Harris, David Edwards, Ken Plummer, Don Allen. Seated: Johnny Gilbert, Marion Holding, Joy Allen, Wendy Rogers, Robin Rogers.

Joan's younger brother John Harris recalled his early life in conversation with his contemporary Don Allen:

> Clothes were handed down from one child to another and no-one ever thought to ask questions about what they wore. Neither boy had a pair of long trousers until he reached his teens. Toys were mostly hand-made by parents. Don had a wooden truck which he pushed for miles, sometimes as far as Yardley or Stoke Park where he would pick bluebells. He even had a light for it so that he could take it out at night. In Grafton in those dark days of the war it was safe for children of eight or nine years old to play out at night. A moonlit night with clouds hurrying across the sky seemed like a good night to climb to the top of the church tower, but just as they stepped out there was a neigh from a nearby horse which terrified them. They ran home that night!

Amusement was homespun. John and Don collected the trays from matchboxes which were slotted together to form a wheel, then pushed something through to form a spindle so that it would turn like the mill

Grafton Regis

45 The children in the village in 2000. Back row, left to right: Louisa Reece, Ella Weston, Nikki Patterson, Anna Lavelle, Helena Reece, Sam Martin, Sarah Castle. Middle row: James Harrod, Ashleigh Harrod, Becky Castle, William Weston. Front row: Cara Drake, Andrew McGrath, George FitzRoy, Nico FitzRoy, Danielle Riley, Victoria Riley.

wheel when placed over the brook. It did not always turn out perfectly, and there are memories of falling into the brook, then lighting a fire in a disused barn to dry clothes, or releasing workmens' boats from the towpath.

Leisure and events

Several villagers recall the central role played by the radio in everyday entertainment in the immediate post-war years. Even the pleasure of listening to the radio, though, was affected by the absence of electricity, as John Harris recalls:

> I remember taking accumulator batteries down to the Manor to be recharged. They had a generator there. We used to listen to programmes on the wireless, like the Bruce Woodcock fight, and as the accumulator ran low we just used to hope the fight would end before the wireless packed up.

Ena and Ted Atkins recall the arrival of television in Grafton, hot on the heels of mains electricity:

> When electricity came to Grafton in 1952, it came to the Lodge first, from the direction of Alderton and then on to Grafton. Ted bought a Pye 9 in. TV in time for the Coronation. Most of the men from the village came up to watch the 1953 Stanley Matthews Cup Final. It broke down on the Thursday before the Saturday, and Goodes delivered it just as the men came in the gate. The men included Cyril Hall, Frank Hall, Chimp, John Faulkner, Don Allen, Mr Richardson from Roade, Ena's Dad, and Mr and Mrs At.

The village pub, the White Hart, was also a social centre for the village, and ran darts and skittles teams—skittles meant table skittles, a relatively local form of the game played with 'cheeses' which knock down the skittles with a terrific crash. During the 1980s a skittles marathon gained the pub a place in the *Guinness Book of Records*. The part of the pub which housed these games is now filled with tables where customers eat. Pete Plummer recalls the darts team in its heyday:

> Fred [Odell] bought a Big Four Norton with a WarAg box sidecar which doubled as transport for the White Hart darts team. I've seen him transport the whole team of seven players on that motorbike and sidecar. Cyril Hall fell off the back once, and Bill Swain slipped off the front, but as they were well oiled they never ever came to any harm.

These were not the only areas of sporting prowess represented in Grafton. Jane Sargeant, who lived all her life in Grafton until she married in 1987, won numerous show-jumping trophies both at home and abroad. She competed with British teams and rode in the winning Nations Cup team in Lisbon in 1983.

Bellringing was a very popular activity in the village. Robin Rogers recalls the bells of St Mary the Virgin being rehung:

> In 1948, the church bells at Grafton were rehung, and a new treble added to make a peal of five bells. This was the result of my Gran (Eunice Olive Allen, née Fennemore) having the idea to rehang the bells in thanksgiving for those who returned safely from the Second World War. She went to see Mrs Annand (the wife of the Rector before the Cartmans) and got an initial donation for the project. The rest of the money was largely raised by whist drives,

lots of which were held at The Bank.

At Grafton on New Year's Eve, we used to cycle to Alderton and ring late evening, then go to the Fountaines' farm for mince pies and port or sherry. That was a wonderful occasion. Then we went to Grafton and rang the bells at midnight to say farewell to the old year and to welcome the new. Bellringers at Grafton were myself, Frank Hall, Cyril Hall, George Atkins, and John Neale, who for a time worked at Allibone's farm. My sister Toni rang, as did the Reverend B.Fernyhough, the Rector. One New Year, Bill Allen and his sons Don and Brian also rang.

There were seasonal activities in the village too. Robin Rogers recalls the village bonfire and the Parish Party:

> Each year there was a village bonfire in the field just past Aunt Joyce's house [opposite Old Barn Cottages]. This was a grand affair. Suitable bonfire material was collected for weeks, and we had sparklers and ate hot chestnuts and roast potatoes. We watched other people's rockets and Catherine wheels, and had the odd banger. One year the bonfire was sabotaged a few days early. The thatch of The Bank was also set alight by a firework.
>
> A big event was the Parish Party, held in the old school. Everyone got very jolly, and it was a fun evening. The bar used to be in the porch at the end, and there was dancing and singing to the piano, which Mum played.

Don Allen and John Harris remember carol singing at the Manor. They would be asked in and would then sing different carols for different members of the family. Jane and Mahala Bagshaw, who spent some of their childhood at Grafton Fields in the 1930s and early 1940s, recall the Manor Christmas party:

> The Christmas Party was another big day in the village. Lady Hillingdon gave the children presents and I received a much-loved doll. I seem to remember going as a fairy, the dress came as a hand-me-down from a rich cousin in London, all gold net with wired wings—Wonderful!

The Grafton Hunt was established around 250 years ago and still meets. Several villagers tell stories related to it. David Edwards tells the following tale which he believes was published as a true story:

In the 1920s the Grafton were justifiably proud of their fox-catching exploits. At the Hunt Ball the local gamekeeper struck a five guinea wager with the Grafton Master that he could breed foxes that the hunt would never catch.

Now the gamekeeper knew where there was a vixen who had recently had cubs and made a point of throwing her the odd rabbit for the cubs. Vic Edwards, aged eight, was sent down the lair and brought up all the cubs to the gamekeeper. The gamekeeper cut off their tails, returned them to the lair, and they learned to run without having to worry about the weight of their brush. When they grew up they ran like the wind and were never caught. The gamekeeper collected his five guineas.

Charles Reece relates the folllowing story told to him by Chimp Richardson:

As a boy, Chimp often saw the Hunt run down near Bozenham Mill. One day, on the road towards Ashton, he saw a fox run across the road and into Mrs Bliss's Backside field. Moments later, the Master of the Hunt came galloping by and seeing Chimp, stopped to ask if he had seen the fox. 'Yes, sir', Chimp replied, 'he's gone up Mrs Bliss's Backside'. As the Master did not know the abbreviated local name for the field, Chimp was told off for his rudeness, and the Hunt went the wrong way!

The village also has a long history of organised entertainment of a less strenuous nature. The Harvest Supper is an institution which continues into the 21st century. Joy Wilson has been the main organiser of the event for some years, with Charles Reece providing his own brand of one-man cabaret.

Charles himself recalls the beginnings of another event, the Medieval Fayre:

In 1977, Grafton celebrated the Silver Jubilee jointly with Alderton, with Alderton people coming to Grafton for the day. After competitions for the best-dressed house and the best hat (won by Mrs Hedley), there was the serious business of the Grafton vs Alderton football match. The afternoon concluded with a meal in Colgroves' barn which went on into the next few days because there was so much food left over.

The success of the Silver Jubilee prompted the organisation of Grafton's first Medieval Fayre in 1978. Originally planned as a rather elaborate fete, the first decent Sunday in the summer brought out well over 1,000 visitors, a far greater than the 200–300 anticipated. The result was chaos; the tea tent couldn't meet the demand for hot water, made worse by the constant fusing of the old copper. The rota for stallholders disintegrated under the demands placed on the helpers and stallholders weren't relieved for the whole of the day. By the end of the afternoon, David Pickering in his wheelchair on car park duty had every pocket stuffed to overflowing with money because nobody had time to relieve him of the whole day's taking. All subsequent fayres were much better organised under the leadership of first Winifred Champion from 1978 to 1981, then jointly with Sue Blake in 1982, and then Sue Blake alone in 1983 and 1984.

The event became very popular. Hundreds of people flocked to the village, parking in the field running down to the canal and walking up to where bands played and games and stalls were set up. A large proportion of the village was involved in some way or another, running stalls, operating games, making and selling refreshments, taking gate money, directing cars in the car park, selling programmes, or in another of the numerous activities involved in the day. An activity etched in the memory is the erection of the marquee on the day before the event, and then of the stalls. Mick Boon delivered the marquee and stalls, and many of the men of the village helped get them into place. The Fayres always took place on Sundays and always attracted wonderful weather.

Sarah and Becky Castle recall a Village Hall event celebrating a specific occasion in the mid 1990s. Sarah writes:

> My sister and I were born and bred in Grafton Regis. Our earliest memory of a village gathering was the VJ Day celebrations at the Village Hall. We helped prepare food in kitchens throughout Grafton all morning (although I think we were more of a hindrance than a help). Together with several other village children, we had a fancy dress competition, complete with evacuees, soldiers and gas masks. After that we had a sing-song, with our rather tipsy 80 year-old grandma singing a Vera Lynn classic. Later, our parents took home some very tired and overfed children. The next morning, our grandmother, like many others, had a bad headache!

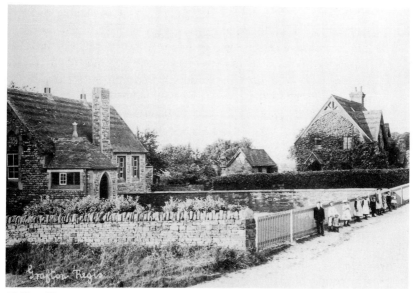

46 The village school in the early years of the 20th century.

Schooling in 20th-century Grafton

The village school continued to serve both Grafton and Alderton after the First World War, until 1923 with the long-serving Mrs Brafield as mistress. In March 1919 the school had to close because there was no coal, and the wood which the boys had been collecting for the previous fortnight had run out. In November 1921 the children observed the Armistice Day silence but Mrs Brafield noted in her log-book that she had decided not to send for any poppies to sell at the school: with fathers' wages much lower than in the past, money was scarce in the two villages.

Following Mrs Brafield's retirement pupil numbers declined and the school closed at Easter 1934. After the closure, the schoolroom became a public hall, which the village had previously lacked. Set against this gain to the community was a feeling, expressed by one Alderton resident in the early 1960s, that the closure of the school, which had tended to bring Grafton Regis and Alderton together, led to the two villages growing apart, since the children now travelled to different schools and saw little of each other. Alderton children went to Paulerspury and those from Grafton to Yardley Gobion. After the war children from Grafton who did not secure selective school places continued to receive all their education at Yardley until 1949, when Yardley was reorganised as an

47 A young Bill Allen outside the school-yard fence.

infant and junior school and children who did not win places at Towcester Grammar School went first to Potterspury, which functioned for a few years as a rudimentary secondary school, or, after it opened in 1958, to the purpose-built Deanshanger Secondary Modern School (now Kingsbrook School). In the 1950s, car owners in Grafton organised a rota to take children to Yardley because of the limitations of the bus service.

Although the information we have about the history of the school is fascinating, it lacks one important element, which is what the schools were like through the eyes of their pupils. We have no recollections from those who attended the pre-1873 school, and very few of that which closed in 1934. Maurice Allen has a particularly vivid memory of an incident at school involving himself and his friend Johnnie Gilbert, who was always known as Billy:

> The teacher was putting up the Christmas decorations at school, paper chains which we had all made, and as she stood on the steps to reach we stood underneath so that we could see her drawers. Billy said they were pink and I said they were white and she overheard us. 'What are you doing?', she asked. 'Looking at your knickers and he says they are pink and I say they are white', I replied. 'Well, you are both wrong because they are green', she announced, and lifted her frock up for all to see, astonishing us because teachers did not do that sort of thing.

Robin Rogers relates a story told by his mother, Jean Rogers, about 'Chimp', Alfred Richardson, at school:

> Mum said that when she was at school at Grafton, the teacher asked who had seen a ship. Allegedly, Chimp raised a hand and said he had seen one 'in Park Close field'. Being interested in sheep, and having a wonderful Northamptonshire accent, it was no doubt considered an appropriate response.

48 Children at Grafton School, *c.* 1926–9. Standing left to right: Johnny Gilbert, Mary Warren, Doris Webb, Joe Allen, Alice Webb, Ted Webb, Mrs Wells (Mistress), Neggy Gollins, Jean Allen, Bill Blunt. Seated: Bob Holloway, Phyllis Allen, Vic Edwards, Maurice Allen, Nancy Holloway, Dorothy Hall, Molly Holding.

Village families and characters

Many of the past and present villagers who have contributed to this part of the book remember characters who lived in the village in earlier times, so we have included a number of their tales in this section. Many of these pen pictures date from around the middle of the 20th century and recall people who were only known to those people who have lived the longest in Grafton. If we move a little closer to the present day, it is possible to recall a host of no less remarkable people, many of whom sadly died in the early 1990s, but who are quite fresh in the memory. When Kathy and I moved to Grafton in 1980, the first person we met was Ursula Holmes, who brought a bunch of roses and introduced herself. Ursula was a wildlife artist living with her husband Clifford at Ivy Cottage. Her career was outlined in an article published in the *Northampton Mercury & Herald* in 1971 reproduced in the CD-ROM. Ursula helped us stock our garden and gave us walnuts and peaches from the trees in her garden. We soon met Chimp, who was by this time living over the road in part of what is now Grove Cottage. I asked him if he had a scythe which I could borrow to cut down the long grass which was all that was growing in the garden. He said he had, that he wouldn't lend it to me, but that he would cut our grass with it, which he did. Chimp, later in company with Nancy, walked up Church Lane at 9 p.m. every night to the White Hart, and claimed to appreciate the light on the outside of our cottage, which to some small extent penetrated the pitch darkness in the lane.

Arch Bushell had retired as landlord of the White Hart some months before we arrived in the village, but he and his wife Bett were living in Church Lane. Tudor Cottage was the home of Alan and Winifred Champion. Alan had coxed the winning Cambridge boat race crew in the last race before the Second World War, had become Warden of Pilgrim's College, Boston, and was a tutor for the Open University. Winifred was heavily involved with the Village Hall Committee and in the organisation of the very successful Medieval Fayres of the late 1970s and early 1980s. Almost next door to Tudor Cottage, at The Beeches, lived the Wilmer family, who ran a photography business in Stony Stratford. In his spare time, Fred flew hot air balloons. One of our earliest memories of living in Grafton is hearing a mighty hissing sound at the back of the house. Before we could investigate, friends arrived who told us that driving up the A508 they had seen a balloon inflating behind our house; soon after, it sailed up and away into the summer evening. Mabel Melsom, the subject of a 1979 *Chronicle & Echo* article on the CD-ROM which describes her first book of poems, lived in The Chantry, and Arthur Coxall lived in The Cabin, opposite Fred Weston. No book on Grafton would be complete without a mention of Fred Weston. For many years, Fred organised the daily paper deliveries to the village, and on Sunday mornings he would come round to collect the money. Always a cheerful character, he would spend a few minutes imparting up-to-the-minute local news. It is unlikely that the paper round made him any money, but Fred was the sort of person who would do this as a service for the village. He was a great fundraiser, and ran all sorts of sweeps and Christmas clubs to raise money for the church and the village hall. Many of these people who lived in Grafton in 1980 had lived here for much of their lives and had a rich and detailed knowledge of the place, but sadly their memories have gone largely unrecorded.

The man who seems to symbolise Grafton Regis is Alfred Richardson, known to all as 'Chimp'. Chimp was a true countryman whose long life, 1907 to 1991, represents a link between the agriculture-based village of previous centuries and the present day. The *Northampton Independent* published an article about him in 1984:

> 'Real' countrymen are getting thin on the ground. By that I mean those who grew up the sons of farm workers in the old days of agriculture, when many still got a meagre living off the land in a

way that now seems hard beyond belief. Such a one is Alfred Jesse Richardson, of 1 Manor Cottages, Grafton Regis. Although an institution in that village, few would identify him by these baptismal names because for reasons long lost he is known to all as 'Chimp'.

He was born at Oundle in 1907 but at the age of six months was brought to Bozenham Mill Farm, where his father was employed as a shepherd. Bozenham Mill stood on the River Tove between Ashton and Grafton certainly since the 13th century but was demolished in the 1950s and scarcely a trace of it exists today. The farm was one of three rented from the Duke of Grafton by 'Master' Bliss, as he was termed, being something of a gentleman farmer.

From the age of five, Chimp was engaged in tasks such as cleaning mangolds, using a sort of miniature bill-hook about a foot long with a spike projecting with which to pick up each root. He still owns one of these and I'm sure that to introduce a modern infant to such a weapon would lead to bloodshed. He also went crow scaring and collecting sparrows' eggs, for which Master Bliss would pay three old pence a score. Rats' tails were also a source of profit, however small, since these creatures nibbled at the fringe of what was still a near subsistence economy.

By the age of 14, Chimp had finished his schooling at Ashton and graduated to being one of several ploughboys employed by Master Bliss. This may sound idyllic, but there was little romance in slogging beside a team of horses across the heavy Northampton-shire claylands. Even then, Bozenham Mill was in decline. A blacksmith's shop and bake house contiguous to the mill still existed but both were out of use, and the mill was only operated for odd sessions of grinding. Eel traps were still in situ and a sheep dip adjacent was in regular use. It was apparently the custom to 'accidentally' drown one animal from every flock so that the men who worked the dip were sure of some good meals of mutton after their labours. Chimp remembers fishing from the Mill House windows and how the mill wheel was renewed for the last time by the father of Albert Shakeshaft, who is still resident at Chapel House, Ashton.

As a boy, among his other farming duties Chimp helped his father drive sheep and cattle to Northampton Market. They used a sapient dog who, when they reached the South Bridge, was despatched home alone. Having delivered their charges to the market, the Richardsons, father and son, would then catch a train from the Castle Station to Roade, walking home from there, at

49 Alfred Jesse ('Chimp') Richardson, probably Grafton's best loved character of the 20th century.

which stage the dog would join them. Another episode, which stays in Chimp's memory from those early years, was when a bull had to be taken for slaughter to Northampton. It was of such massive dimensions that no cart could contain it, so that Richardson senior led it on a pole attached to its nose-ring every step of the way, the copper ring still being in Chimp's possession.

Father Richardson was a shepherd all his working days, and in 1930 Chimp took up the same vocation at Grafton Lodge Farm. This was in the ownership of the Martin family—the firm of Henry Martin then being a very large and prosperous building enterprise. Since they also had further grazing ground at Wootton, the young shepherd was constantly traversing the roads and lanes between these villages and Northampton.

He knew as individuals the 1,400 sheep in his care. He recalls the disappearance of one 'yow' (as he termed it, meaning a ewe) from a field by Toll Gate Cottage and its mysterious re-appearance miles away at Yardley Gobion. One particularly eccentric Suffolk yow brought forth twins annually but when they were born bit off their tails. This might seem of no account, but in fact hit Chimp's pocket. In those days, no-one had heard of unsocial hours of working, but the shepherd got some recompense for his constant duty at lambing-time by the payment of 'three ha'pence'—one and a half old pennies—for the tail of each lamb which survived until they were docked. To avoid this loss of threepence, Chimp used to dip the tails of these particular lambs in carbonized oils to deter the over-zealous mother.

After six years of shepherding, Chimp decided there were easier ways of making a living and went to work for J.S. Cowley & Son, a firm of builders and undertakers still flourishing at Stony Stratford. The outbreak of the Second World War resulted in his working on Government contracts at Whaddon and Hanslope Park and he moved into Civil Service employment at the latter. He had never married and was still living with his parents—they had moved by then to Grafton—when in 1950 his father retired and asked him to take over his job on the Wakefield Estate. This he did and continued in it until his own retirement from full-time work at the age of 65. In doing so he sacrificed the chance of a Civil Service pension, but says he has no regrets. He certainly appears a happy man despite being plagued by shingles, a most discomforting complaint.

He is full of anecdotes from the old days. For a number of years he was one of a quartet of stalwarts who 'shouldered' the coffins of the locals on their last journey to the churchyard. Bowler hats were worn and grew ancient in the service. They were laid on the grass for the later stages of the ceremony, so that when one was trodden on the excuse was made that its colour made it indistinguishable from its background where it lay.

Preoccupation with mortality was then a characteristic of rural life—not like today when death is almost a dirty word—and Chimp has a number of stories on this theme. His mother once went with another woman to lay out an old man who was well into his nineties. They stripped off the bedclothes to begin their task but got a nasty shock when the 'corpse' sat up and intoned: 'Cor—I AM cold!'

Other old villagers come back to life in Chimp's reminiscences, from the time when Grafton was mostly peopled by country folk of the old school. One ancient man asked him to put down his cat when it was nearing its end. Following the custom of that day, the moggy was popped into a weighted sack and dropped into the nearby Grand Union Canal. His mission accomplished, Chimp was taken aback when the late cat's owner asked for the return of the sack!

Not so long ago you could walk into many country inns and find a group of men such as Chimp talking of days gone by. Few of them had ever got more than a pittance from their labours, but from their life and work they had distilled the wisdom of the fields and could make intelligent and entertaining conversation. They have no successors. The minute modern farming force are unlikely to cull anecdotes from the behaviour of such things as tractors and combine harvesters.

In 1980, Lou Warwick's Out and About column in the *Northampton Independent* described his many years of Sunday visits to the White Hart, his friendship with regulars such as Jerry Rogers, George Holding, Ray Carter and Ted Reece, and his discovery that their lives were not by any means totally bound up with Grafton. The article, the full text of which is on the Grafton CD-ROM, includes a moving account of the last months of one of these notable Grafton characters, Ted Reece, who died of motor neurone disease in 1973. In common with several members of the Plummer family who came to live in the village in the 1940s, Ted was a semi-professional musician. He who formed his own band, known as the Carlton Players and later The Ted Reece Band. With son Charles, Ted's widow Hylda participated in the final Dunkirk reunion in June 2000; Ted was amongst the British forces evacuated from Dunkirk,

50 'Off to War'. An optimistic First World War scene in front of The Bank on the main road.

relieved to get away from the European mainland, but heartbroken because he had taken all his beloved sheet music with him and had to leave it all behind. After Dunkirk Ted played mainly by ear.

We have collected many stories and pieces of information about village characters, some of whom, like Granny Allen, appear frequently throughout this section of the book. The following accounts and anecdotes feature people who are mentioned less frequently if at all, but are nonetheless interesting.

Before the First World War, George Atkins (known with his wife as Mr and Mrs At) worked at Isworth Farm near Yardley Gobion and left to work at Bozenham Mill for 6d. per week more. Mr At also worked at Grafton Lodge before the First World War, and Mr Martin said that all those who left the Lodge to go to the war would have a job when they came back. Mr At served at Gallipoli and told Charles Reece of the story of his retreat there. They left behind a few guns with strings attached between the triggers and empty cans. Water from a barrel was allowed to drip into the can so that after a while the guns would go off randomly to give them more time to escape. Mr At was demobbed and got the train to Wolverton, walking all the way home to the Grafton area and starting work the next day. Although he went back to Grafton Lodge, he later went to Maple Farm, Collingtree, to work

51 Left: Violet Newberry (on the right) as a First World War Land Army girl from Alderton. Popularly known as 'Mrs At', she was Grafton's Sunday School teacher between 1947 and 1961. Right: George Atkins at Grafton Lodge in the 1920s. George worked at the farm before and after the First World War and again after the Second War. His name appears on the plaques marking the various peals that were rung at the church after 1945.

for Sears. By a twist of fate, Henry (Harry) Sargeant bought Maple in 1942 and then Grafton Lodge in 1946. He then asked Mr At to come back and manage Grafton Lodge, which he did until 1961.

Tom Elliott (uncle of Mrs Ward of Piddington, who contributed this information) was farm manager for the Martins at Grafton Lodge between the wars and originally lived at the Lodge until the red brick cottage was built for him in the 1920s. Tom married Ellen (Nell) and had a daughter Edith Mabel (known as Mabel) who was 12 when she went to the Lodge. Since she was 42 when she died in 1943, then Tom must have moved to Grafton Lodge just before the First World War.

Mabel Elliott was a great photographer and took many pictures at this time. She courted Leslie Chapman, son of Henry and Bertha at the White Hart. Leslie died in hospital on 19 May 1924, aged 30, following a motorbike accident between Grafton and Northampton. Mabel was unable to get to the hospital before Leslie died. For the rest of her short life she suffered poor health due to asthma. Tom Elliott lived to be 90 and is buried with his wife

52 Tom Elliott as a young man. Tom was farm manager at Grafton Lodge during the Second World War and discovered the petrified Irishmen in Park Close. He later told the ghost story to Joe Sargeant in 1947.

Ellen and daughter Mabel in Grafton churchyard, although Mabel's name is not clear on the headstone. Leslie Chapman is buried nearby.

Do you remember Fred Odell who lived in a hut behind the church where Millstones is now? One day his geese were all painted blue and he thought I had done it, but it was really David Edwards and Peter Plummer. Fred was a bit of a character. He was keen on motorbikes. At one time he had two but he had only one number plate which he used to switch between them. (John Harris)

There was a lady in the village called Marge Rogers who was 'not quite the ticket', being in the habit of going for walks, usually holding a handbag up to her face and sometimes walking backwards, 'just for a change'. She would then stop and board a bus from wherever she happened to be for a few miles and then get off without ever paying any fare. She was known to all the bus crews. Marge lived in Rosebud Cottage on the Main Road and on one occasion during the war she put all her rugs out into the middle of the road in order to brush them and refused to move away until she had finished although she was holding up an Army convoy. (Don Allen and John Harris)

The Frosts lived in Norfolk Cottage, almost opposite. They were both very old when I was a small child. I remember Mr Frost used to keep pigs. He had an old sow nearly as big as a donkey, probably as old as him. He bred piglets from it every year for years, and when he eventually sold the sow my mother would not buy any pork for weeks for fear it might be from the old sow. There was a joke at the time that he had a cat which lived in the sty and for which he had cut a hole to give it access. When the cat had kittens he had a small hole cut for the kittens. (Maurice Allen)

Mr Frowhawk was at The Manor where he ran a choir school with an Abyssinian gentleman, Mr DeLouis. The Chantry was unoccupied, Mr Frowhawk used to keep chickens in there. He also kept chickens in the Manor ballroom. He also kept a few cows. There were two little Persian children there, a boy and a girl who appeared to be very badly exploited, treated almost like slaves. They used to milk the cows and would often take them down the lane to graze on the grass verge. Mr Frowhawk eventually went bananas, having his grand piano put out on to the front lawn and, after playing some classical piece on it, set fire to it. He was a brilliantly clever man and did some good things for the church. Before moving to Grafton we came over to a midnight service in the church on Christmas Eve and the choir from the school sang.

He also installed lighting into the church. (John and Margaret Colgrove)

There were two brick cottages in Church Lane on the left as you go towards the church. The far end one was occupied by a lovely man named Blunt who was for years a gardener at the Manor and in the other one lived a Mr and Mrs Brown. When I was a very small child [in the 1920s], Mrs Brown cut her throat, and then tried to drown herself in the water butt. That was the big story at the time. He was a very smart old man who used to grow beautiful roses. The garden where he lived had a path to it from the field by the horse chestnut tree which was the back way into his cottage and he always had that full of standard roses. They were absolutely gorgeous. He really knew how to grow them, budding and grafting them himself. (Maurice Allen)

We have some interesting brief insights into the life of the Green family from Mrs Green of Roade:

The family moved to Grafton Fields in 1935, a farm owned by the Grafton estate and farmed by Mr Bagshaw. Dick's father Percy worked as a farm labourer for Mr Bagshaw and lived in part of the main house. Dick recalls George V's Silver Jubilee celebrations in the May. Percy went to school at Yardley Gobion and soon started work at Pianoforte Supplies in Roade, cycling daily to and from work. Dick still worked in Northampton, six days a week. His journey to work started with a cycle ride to Roade to catch a workers' bus to Northampton in order to start work at 7.30 a.m. At night, the journey was reversed with Dick arriving home at 7 p.m. just in time for dinner. Life was mostly work and sleep having to get up so early.

Most of our recollections of village characters are largely anecdotal, but a great deal of meticulous genealogical work based on documentary evidence has been done on one of Grafton's longest-standing families, the Addingtons. Sheila Jelley has written an introduction to her family history of the Addingtons. This is an extract:

My first visit to Grafton Regis was in the late 1950s when I visited with my fiancé Colin Jelley, whose mother Beatrice (1911–65) regularly visited the birthplace of her father George William Addington. The family have several photographs taken in Grafton, especially of Mrs Morton, who lived in one of the cottages which are now Grove Cottage. Over the years, my husband and I have visited Grafton Regis with his aunt Dorothy Rich (née Addington), and have on many occasions been seen clearing the graves of George Walter Addington and his wife Mary Ann (née Adams) and their unmarried daughter Mary Ann Addington, which are situated behind the Church as you enter from Church Lane.

In editing extracts from Sheila Jelley's extensive record of the Addington family between 1774 and 1923, I have tried to move backwards in time, beginning with George William Addington, to whom Mrs Morton is believed to have been nursemaid in part of what is now Grove Cottage. George William had been baptised in St Mary the Virgin, Grafton Regis, on 10 March 1878. He moved to Crouch Hill, London, in the 1890s, where he ran a ham and beef business, married Louisa Elizabeth Chinner and had seven children. George William maintained strong links with Grafton throughout his life; on occasion he would hire a car and drive the family out from London for a visit. George William and Louisa's eldest son George James Addington was killed in 1918 in France, where his name is listed on the Pozières War Memorial as well as on the memorial in St Mary the Virgin.

George William Addington was the sixth of ten children born to George Walter Addington, who was baptised at St Mary the Virgin on 25 December 1835, and Mary Ann Adams. George William's father, George Walter, who worked as an agricultural labourer, was in turn the second of seven children born to Abraham Addington (1806–72), also an agricultural labourer, and Anne Johnson (1808–90), who were married at St Mary the Virgin in 1826. Anne appears to have been a remarkable woman. She is said to have walked with the pram in her younger days to visit her parents in Hollowell, north of Northampton! All seven children were baptised at Grafton Regis. The eldest of the seven, Catherine (baptised 30 May 1830), made an unhappy match. She married Richard Woodward, a boatman, in St Mary the Virgin on 26 February 1851, although at the time of the Census the following month she was living with her parents. The couple lived in Stoke Bruerne and had nine children. One day, Catherine was found crying on the side of the road with her young baby by a local farmer named Savage, who stopped and offered her one of his cottages for the remainder of her life. Catherine died in Stoke Bruerne in 1908. Descendants of this marriage live in Australia and one, Peter Hawkins, has undertaken a good deal of work on the family's history. There is also another Australian link. Abraham's sister Rosanna Addington married James Smith in Grafton and then moved to Northampton. Their great-great-great-granddaughter Judy

Beattie lives in Melbourne and is yet another person who has undertaken extensive work on her family history.

Sheila Jelley writes that she always feels sad when she reads about the history of Abraham's brother John, who was baptised on 6 November 1808 and married Sophia Lever at Potterspury on 24 December 1832. John was killed in June 1837 at Ashton when he was working on building the railway embankment, and Sophia died of a decline two years later. They had three children, of whom the eldest, William, was baptised at St Mary the Virgin on 23 June 1833. William was in the workhouse at Yardley Gobion in 1841, at Passenham schoolhouse in 1851, and was then a gardener at Ashton. He committed suicide on 23 May 1911 in Grafton Regis and is buried in the churchyard. John and Sophia's second child Martha was baptised in St Mary the Virgin on 19 April 1835 and was buried in May 1835. The third child Henry Abraham was baptised on 31 May 1837 in St Mary the Virgin, seven days before his father John was buried there. Henry was in the Yardley Gobion workhouse with his elder brother William in 1841 and was there on his own in 1851. The 1861 Census records that Henry had found work as a shoemaker and was living in Hanslope with his niece Matilda Jane Abbot. He subsequently moved to Louth (Lincs.), where he died unmarried in 1914.

Abraham Addington's parents were William Addington and Maria Chaplin, who were married in Stoke Goldington on 2 September 1798, lived in Grafton Regis, and had eight children, one of whom died in infancy. Abraham was the fourth born. William Addington, Abraham's father, was an agricultural labourer. We know a little more about him than about most of his contemporaries in Grafton since in 1811 he was charged with stealing 14 hogs, the property of John Smith of Potterspury Lodge. Then in 1817 he was imprisoned for having milked five cows and carried away the milk, the property of Thomas Warr of the White Hart, Grafton Regis.

William was the fourth child of ten born to Thomas Addington and Martha Craft, at least three of whom died in infancy. Thomas, an agricultural labourer working on the Duke of Grafton's estate, married Martha on 5 November 1774 in St Mary the Virgin, where all their children were also baptised. Thomas represents the starting point for Sheila Jelley's family history.

The work which has been done on the history of the Addington family, of which more appears on the Grafton CD-ROM, is invaluable to Grafton in a number of ways. So far as this book is concerned, it gives us vivid insights into the daily lives of people who spent their lives in the village, which is the kind of history which normally disappears unrecorded. The lives of the Addingtons also illustrate several features of life in Grafton which have changed dramatically. For example, very large families are much less common than they were up until the beginning of the 20th century, nor do so many children die in infancy. Although the number of houses in Grafton has not changed significantly, the number of people living in each one is generally very much smaller. Finally, it is also much more common nowadays for young members of the family to leave the village to find work and to live in another part of the country or even in another part of the world. The patterns of life of the Addington family and of other families like them in Grafton and across England have disappeared for ever.

Conclusion

We have tried in this chapter to present a picture of day-to-day life in Grafton Regis throughout the 20th century. This has not been easy because few useful printed records are available and because many of the people who knew Grafton at the beginning of the century have sadly died and taken their memories with them. Nevertheless, we have been very fortunate to receive a wide variety of recollections and impressions from past and present villagers, many more than we could include in the book, which is built upon short extracts from these accounts. We hope to have given a flavour of village life which will tempt you to explore further by investigating the Grafton CD-ROM, which will contain many more stories and illustrations than could be included in the book. The CD-ROM will be published in 2001.

APPENDICES

1. Grafton Regis Constable's Account

Though the losses may have been exaggerated as they formed a claim for compensation, this account (Public Record Office, SP 28/171, ff. 31–6) illustrates the impact of a military force quartered for a few days on a small village. With the help of the 1650 survey it is possible to identify most of the houses. Marthana Wilson ran the King's Arms, which explains the large quantity of malt, Richard Wardly held a substantial farm, while Ann Goodman occupied two farms and John Atterbury another. Edward Foster and Peter Brown had been alehouse keepers in 1630, the latter also the blacksmith who had a cottage on the Northampton road. Richard Chapman and Thomas Bell also each held a cottage. Only eight of the 17 tenants listed in 1650 claimed losses; two who did claim, Richard James and John Fearnsley, are not in the survey.

Taken awaye by Maior Generall Skiptons Armie of the *Ladie Cranes personal Estate at Grafton Regis 1643*	£	s.	d.
2 sadle horses worth	10	00	00
3 carthorses worth	15	00	00
8 milk cows & fatt heffers	32	00	00
Lady Crane's estate in money Plate household stuffe corne and haye to the vallue of	5000	00	00
Taken awaye and caried to Northampton 300 hunded weight of lead and great store of iron work	20	00	00

Mrs Marthana Willsons estate Taken away at the same seidge of Grafton House *by Maior General Skiptons armie*			
In Malt 56 quarters	68	00	00
40 sheepe	20	00	00
Linnan and other goods worth	40	00	00

from Ann Goodman at the same time 1643 at Grafton			
1 hogshead of beer	00	13	04
Bread, meat and other provisions	00	10	00
Poultrie as henns and geese	01	01	06
Pease and corne eaten and spoyled	02	10	10
Haye and strawe	01	10	00
Brasse and other houshold stuffe worth	02	02	06
Iron taken away to Cutt to shoot(e)	01	10	08
2 hives of Beese	00	13	04
1 horse worth	05	10	00
fier wood burned	01	06	08
Ann Goodman hir mark			

From Richard Chapman at the same time Anno 1643			
2 hogsheads of beare worth	02	00	00

159

Bread meat and other provisions	00	10	00
A fatt porket	00	06	00
firewood burned in the house and in the park	07	00	00
pease on the hovells	01	00	00
Brasse and pewter worth	01	00	00
Iorne houusehold stuffe worth	00	06	00

Provisons Maior Generall Skiptons Armie had of Richard Wardly both for men and horse and other things Anno 1643:

Item in Bread, meat and flower to the vallue of	01	04	00
3 hundred waight of Cheese	06	00	00
50 pounde of powdred Butter	00	18	09
2 hogsheds a barell and 3 kindlots(?) of beer	02	16	00
A greate wood bottle and 9 leather botles	01	00	00
dried Backon 2 flitches	02	00	00
20 pounde of lard	00	10	00
a fat hoge	02	10	00
a store hogge	01	03	04
A fatt Calfe	00	10	00
29 live shepe	10	10	00
poultrie as hens ducks and geese	01	14	00
Beefe and other meate bought agaynst the time	00	12	00
A strike of Oate meale	00	05	04
A strike of Salt	00	04	00
20 strike of Aples	01	00	00
frute and spice	01	10	00
a new hearecloth for a malt kill	00	18	06
9 sax and 2 bagis	01	02	00
2 loade of haye	01	00	00
2 loade of strawe	00	10	00
2 strike of beanes	00	05	04
5 strike of wheate at 4/-	01	00	00
7 quarter and a strike of baorily	07	02	08
8 stocks(?) of Befe at 8/- a peece	03	04	00
A new Carte and a newe pairw of wheeles to Carye the Carage away	05	00	00
2 Set of harnise for 5 horsis with all furniture belonging to them	05	00	00
A younge mare put into the same gearis to helpe to drawe the Carages	05	06	08
Iron to be Cutt to shoote and other tools for husbandmens use of all sorts worth	04	06	08
Brasse and pewter worth	16	00	00
3 Chests and 2 boxes of linnan	15	08	00
3 feather beds and a flock bed with bedcloathes which went away with hart(?) people	12	10	00
28 pound of woolen yarn	01	12	08
57 pound of hemp teere(?)	01	08	06

Wearing apparell of all sorts of Richard Wardleys his wives
  and sonns worth   26   00   00
Bybles and other books worth   05   00   00
fire wood and plow timber and pales burned there   03   00   00
provisons Collonel Brownes men had going by towards
  Abbington   03   08   00
A black mare taken away at the same timeby them   03   00   00
Richard Wardley

**provisons and other things Maior Generall Skiptons Armie had Anno 1643 of
Edward Fostar alias warde**

Item in wine as much as was worth   10   00   00
in beare as much as was worth   12   00   00
vargis(?) worth   03   00   00
Meate and other victualls worth   02   12   00
Beefe worth   03   00   00
Fatt beasts   17   10   00
Sheep   06   10   00
Hogs   06   00   00
weareing Apparell worth   05   10   00
Linnan worth   20   00   00
Bedding worth   10   00   00
17 ells of greene cloth worth   02   00   00
A Carpitt and a Cubbard cloth   00   13   04
Curtines worth   02   00   00
Pewter and brasse worth   05   00   00
Hay worth   12   10   00
Beanes and oats   02   10   00
Fier wood Burned   12   00   00
Joyners tooles worth   05   00   00
Boards worth   06   00   00
2 horses worth   06   00   00

quartering 26 horse and men of Captine Pichfords Troope
  2 dayes 26th and 27th Jan 1645   01   19   00
Edward Foster

Provisons and other things Maior Generall Skiptons Armie had of John Atterburie

2 hogshead of beare   01   10   00
bread and other provisons in the house   01   10   00
12 strike of beanes at 2/8d. per strike   01   12   00
Rawe mault worth   01   10   00
Linnan worth   13   06   08
Poultrie of all sorts worth   00   13   06
2 hillings(?) worth   02   00   00
3 blankets worth   00   15   00
to Redeeme 2 Cowes and a bull at Newporte cost   03   00   00
10 sheepe   02   10   00

4 mares and geldings	23	00	00
weareing Aparell	06	13	04
Brasse and pewter	03	00	00

John Atterburie his mark

Provisons and other things Maior Generall Skiptons Armie had of Peter Browne

3 hogsheads of Ale	03	00	00
2 fatt hogs	03	00	00
Bread meate and other provisons	01	00	00
Brasse and Pewter	04	00	00
A Fether bed a pair of blankes a shiling and 6 pair of sheets	07	00	00
Weareing Aparel of all sorts	02	00	00
In the Smythey the Coales Iorn and Tooles	04	00	00
Fiere wood burned	02	13	04
4 load of Straw	01	06	08

Peter Browne his marke

Of Thos Bell

Brass and Pewter worth	05	00	00
all manner of linnan	02	10	00
Bedding and wearing aparell	03	10	00
in Reddie monney	05	00	00
To Redeeme 2 Cowes at Newport Cost	02	00	00
Beefe and vittuals in the house	01	00	00
Woollen worth	02	00	00

Thomas Bell his marke

Of Richard James

Bread bere and other provisons in the house worth	01	00	00
3 strike of pease	00	08	00
4 live Sheepe	00	15	00
10 hives of beese	04	00	00
wearing Aparell of all sortes	05	08	00
Linnan of all sorts	01	10	00
Brasse and Pewter worth	01	04	00
Bedding of all sortes	01	05	00
18 pounde of woollen reddie Culloured	00	18	00

Richard James his marke

Of John Fearnsley

victuals in his house worth	00	02	00
4 hens and a Cock	00	03	00
Linnan of all sorts worth	01	00	00
Iron ware	00	05	00
Wooden vessell worth	00	02	08

John Fearnsley his marke

2. Rectors of Grafton

	William de Bray	1698	Humphrey Drake
1282	John de Grinstead	1721	John Austin
1288	Simon de Bray	1765	Robert Harding
1333	William de Beaumilla	1792	John Bright
1334	Mr John de Northflete	1833	Frederick Thomas William
1335	Mr John atte Gote (acolyte)		Coke FitzRoy
1335	Peter de Columber	1837	Barwick John Sams
	William atte Wood	1886	Charles James Perne
1373	Phillip de Catesby		Blundell
1387	John de Lyndale	1892	Henry Edwin Barnacle
	Henry Trevylars	1895	Richard Coad Pryor
1438	John Boolde	1901	Alexander Walter Annaud
1442	John Laybourne	1912	Edwin David Annand
1462	Mr Thomas Leeson	1923	Jacob Thompson
1471	Sir Thomas Rawlyns	1926	Robert Noble Beasley
1477	Sir James Molyneux	1936	Grotius Alexander James
1484	Sir John Lambard	1939	Horace Bertram Cartman
1535	William Ingmanthorpe	1953	Guy Marshall
1553	Edward Bune	1957	Ernest Edwin Goodman
1564	John Cruar	1961	Bernard Fernyhough
1575	Lawrence Thorley	1967	Martin Marker Bowen
1578	Anthony Greenacres	1973	Lawrence Wood
1597	John Ibbotson	1978	Jack Higham
1604	Thomas Watson	1983	Hedley Arthur Mitchell
1610	William Piles		Pickard
1612	Thomas Austen	1993	Robert Philip Cave (interreg-
1640	Thomas Bunning		num)
1655	William Paine	1999	John Malcolm Courtie
1681	William Harrison		

Sources: The pre-1541 names are taken from Baker, *History of Northamptonshire*, ii, pp. 177–8; from 1541 to 1833 his list has been checked against H. Isham Longden, *Northants. and Rutland Clergy* (1938–52) and as far as possible the date given is that of institution; more recent names and dates are from *Crockford's Clerical Directory*.

In 1774, during the incumbency of Robert Harding, the rectory of Alderton was annexed to that of Grafton Regis, where ministers resided. In 1954, during the incumbency of Guy Marshall, the rectory of Grafton Regis with Alderton was united with that of Stoke Bruerne, where ministers subsequently resided.

3: Lords of the Manor

1066	Godwin
1086	Robert, Count of Mortain
c. 1091	William, Count of Mortain
By 1106	Abbey of Nôtre-Dame de Grestain, France
1348–50	Tideman de Lymbergh
1354	Sir Michael de la Pole, 1st Earl of Suffolk
1389	William de la Pole
1390	Richard de la Pole
1404	Thomas de la Pole
1421	Thomas de la Pole
1430	William de la Pole, 4th Earl of Suffolk
1440	Richard Woodville, later 1st Earl Rivers
1469	Anthony Woodville, Baron Scales and 2nd Earl Rivers
1483	Richard Woodville, 3rd Earl Rivers
1491	Thomas Grey, 1st Marquess of Dorset
1501	Thomas Grey, 2nd Marquess of Dorset
1527	King Henry VIII

By an Act of Parliament of 1542 the manor of Grafton was created an honor and a number of other manors in Northamptonshire were annexed to the honor.

1547	King Edward VI
1553	Queen Mary
1558	Queen Elizabeth I
1603	King James I
1610	Henry Frederick, Prince of Wales (died 1612)
1612	Charles, Prince of Wales, later King Charles I
1649	King Charles I executed
1660	King Charles II
1665	Queen Catherine of Braganza
1705	Charles FitzRoy, 2nd Duke of Grafton
1757	Augustus Henry FitzRoy, 3rd Duke of Grafton
1811	George Henry FitzRoy, 4th Duke of Grafton
1844	Henry FitzRoy, 5th Duke of Grafton
1863	William Henry FitzRoy, 6th Duke of Grafton
1882	Augustus Charles Lennox FitzRoy, 7th Duke of Grafton
1918	Alfred William Maitland FitzRoy, 8th Duke of Grafton
1930	John Charles William FitzRoy, 9th Duke of Grafton
1936	Charles Alfred Euston FitzRoy, 10th Duke of Grafton
1970	Hugh Denis Charles FitzRoy, 11th Duke of Grafton

BIBLIOGRAPHY

General

Northamptonshire Record Office: Grafton Collection. This extensive family and estate archive forms the basis of the account of the estate since 1706.

Baker, G., *The History and Antiquities of the County of Northampton* (1822–34).

Bridges, J., *The History and Antiquities of Northamptonshire* (1791).

Early History

Aerial Photographs: RAF CPE UK 1994, 1074, 13 April 1947. Cambridge University Collection, 17WN 57, 58.

Published sources: *Northamptonshire Archaeology*, 15, 1980, 171-2; *CBA Group 9 Newsletter*, 10, 1980, p. 32; Dugdale, Sir William, *Monasticon Anglicanum* (1830); Parker, Geoffrey, *The Medieval Hermitage of Grafton*, Survey Report by the Royal Commission on Historical Monuments of England, 1964.

Edward IV and Elizabeth Woodville

Clive, Mary M., *This Sun of York: A Biography of Edward IV* (Macmillan, 1973).

Commines, Philippe de, *Memoires* (3 vols., ed. J.L.A. Calmette and G. Durville, Paris, 1824–5; ed. and trans. M. Jones, Penguin Classics, 1972).

The Croyland Chronicle Continuation, 1459–1486 (ed. N. Prona and J. Cox) (Alan Sutton, 1986).

Fabyan, Robert, *The Cocordance of Histories: The New Chronicles of England and France* (ed. H. Ellis, 1811).

Fahy, C., 'The Marriage of Edward IV and Elizabeth Woodville: a new Italian Source', *English Historical Review*, LXXVI (1960).

'Gregory's Chronicle': The Historical Collections of a Citizen of London in the Fifteenth Century (ed. James Gairdner) (Camden Society, 1876).

Hall, Edward. *The Union of the Two Noble and Illustre Families of Lancaster and York* (ed. H. Ellis (1809; facsimile ed. 1970).

Holinshed, Raphael, *Chronicles* (ed. H. Ellis) (1807).

Holinshed, Raphael, *Chronicles* (ed. Hooker) (1587).

Lander, J.R., *The Wars of the Roses* (1965).

Lander, J.R., *Crown and Nobility, 1450–1509* (1976).

MacGibbon, D., *Elizabeth Woodville* (1938).

Mancini, Dominic, *De Occupatione Regni Anglie per Riccardum Tercium* (trans. and ed. C.A.J. Armstrong (2nd ed., 1969).

Monstrelet, Enguerrand de, *Chroniques d'Enguerran de Monstrelet* (ed. L.Douet d'Arcq) (Paris, 1857–62).

More, Sir Thomas, *The History of King Richard the Third* (1525).

Ross, Charles, *Edward IV* (1974).

Vergil, Polydore, *The Anglica Historia of Polydore Vergil, A.D. 1485–1573* (trans. and ed. D. Hay) (Camden Series, 1950).

Vergil, Polydore, *Three Books of Polydore Vergil's English History* (ed. H. Ellis) (Camden Society, 1844).

Weir, Alison, *Lancaster and York. The Wars of the Roses* (1995).

Henry VIII

Castillon and Charles de Marillac, *Correspondence politique de Castillon and de Marillac, ambassadeurs en Angleterre, 1537–1542* (1885).

Cavendish, George, *The Life and Death of Thomas Wolsey* (1557).

Colvin, H.M., Ransome, D.R., and Summerson, J., *The History of the King's Works. Vol. III, 1485–1660* (1975).

Scarisbrick, J.J., *Henry VIII* (1968).

Singer, Samuel Weller, *The Life of Cardinal Wolsey by George Cavendish* (1827).

Elizabeth I and James I

Erickson, Carolly, *The First Elizabeth* (1983).

Dovery, Zileh, *An Elizabethan Progress* (1998).

Fraser, Antonia, *James I* (1974).

Jenkins, Elizabeth, *Elizabeth and Leicester* (1961).

Letters of King James VI and I (ed. G.P.V. Akrigg) (1984).

The Civil War Siege

Kay, T., *The Story of the Grafton Portrait of William Shakespeare with an Account of the Sack and Destruction of the Manor House of Grafton Regis* (1914).

Whetham, C.D. and W.C.D., *A History of the Life of Colonel Nathaniel Whetham* (1907).

Goldberg, A., *A Short History of Grafton Regis* (1907).

Phillips, I.G. (ed.), *The Journal of Sir Samuel Luke* (Oxfordshire Record Society, xxix–xxxi, 1952–3).

Hall, D., *The Open Fields of Northamptonshire* (Northants. Record Society, xxxviii 1995).

Pettit, P., *The Royal Forests of Northamptonshire* (NRS, xxii, 1969).

Morris, J., *Heaven's Command*, 1973.

Contemporary Newsletters: *Special Passages and Certain Informations from Several Places* (24–31 Jan. 1643); *The True Informer*, 21–28 Oct. 1643; *The Happy Successe of the Parliaments Armie at Newport and some other places*, 10 Nov. 1643; *Parliament Scout*, 10–17 Nov. 1643; *The Parliament Scout*, 17–24 Nov. 1643; *The True Informer*, 18–25 Nov. 1643.; *Remarkable Passages*, 25 Nov. 1643; *The Compleate Intelligencer and Resolver*, 14 Nov. 1643; *The Weekly Account*, 15–22 Nov. 1643; *Mercurius Civicus* 21–28 Dec. 1643; *Remarkable Passages*, 22 Dec. 1643; *A true Relation of the taking of Grafton House by the Parliaments forces, under the Command of Sergeant Major Skipton*. 29 Dec. 1643; *The Parliament Scout*, 22–29 Dec. 1643; *The Weekly Accompt*, 28 Dec. 1643–3 January 1644; *The Parliament Scout*, 29 Dec. 1643–5 Jan. 1644.

Archival sources: Parliamentary Surveys, 1649–50 (Public Record Office, E 317/Northants. 20, 23); Survey of the honor of Grafton, 1660 (Northants. Record Office, G 3199); Survey of the manor of Grafton, 1525–6 (PRO, E 36/179); Alehouse recognisances, 1630, 1672-4 (NRO, FH 2962, QSR1/69/93, Q1/73/124).

INDEX